All glories to Sri Guru and Sri Gauranga

In the Light of Loving Devotion

Srila Bhakti Raksak Sridhar Dev-Goswami Maharaj

With contemporary endnote explanations by
Sripad Bhakti Swarup Tridandi Maharaj

Sri Chaitanya Saraswat Math
London Chapter
Bhakti Yoga Institute
Greville House, Hazelmere Close,
Feltham, TW14 9PX
www.scsmathlondon.org
www.bhaktiyogainstitute.com
www.scsmath.com

Compiled and commented by: Swami B.S. Tridandi
Assistant editors: Suvasini Devi Dasi
Jaya Govinda Prabhu
Chandrika Devi Dasi
Cover artwork: Munindra Mohan Prabhu
Prepared for output: B.R. Madhusudan

ISBN: 978-1-7384093-1-0

Published, printed, and bound in the United Kingdom
by Sri Chaitanya Saraswat Math.
Sri Gaura-Purnima, 25th March 2024.

Śrīla Guru Mahārāj, Oṁ Viṣṇupād
Śrīla Bhakti Rakṣak Śrīdhar Dev-Goswāmī Mahārāj,
whose discourses make up this holy book.

Oṁ Viṣṇupād
Śrīla Bhakti Sundar Govinda Dev-Goswāmī Mahārāj,
Successor Sevāite-President-Āchārya of
Śrī Chaitanya Sāraswat Maṭh.

Oṁ Viṣṇupād
Śrīla Bhakti Rakṣak Śrīdhar Dev-Goswāmī Mahārāj,
Founder-President-Āchārya of
Śrī Chaitanya Sāraswat Maṭh.

Oṁ Viṣṇupād
Śrīla Bhakti Siddhānta Saraswatī Prabhupād,
Founder-Āchārya of Śrī Gauḍīya Maṭh.

Contents

Acknowledgements

Any result is the product of not a single but of several factors, and this book owes its existence to the kind input and assistance of many persons. We would like to acknowledge the following devotees: Rāmānanda Prabhu provided the archive from which the material was drawn and compiled, and Suvāsinī Devī typed the manuscript and assisted in the corrections. She was helped by Jaya Govinda Prabhu, and by Chandrikā Devī and her mother Mrs. Molly-Daniels-Tipping. Paramānanda Prabhu and Lalita Mādhava Prabhu gave useful suggestions. There were many others also who helped along the way – your assistance practically, and in encouraging the project, was invaluable. We offer pranāms also to His Holiness B.R. Madhusūdan Mahārāj and his associates for kindly undertaking the printing and publication. Finally, we ask the kind reader to forgive any mistakes herein which are probably our own.

Praying for the blessings of all the Vaiṣṇavas,

B.S. Tridaṇḍi Swāmī

Lalitā Saptamī, Appearance day of Śrī Lalitā Devī.

22nd September 2023

Foreword

We are honoured to have the opportunity to present the teachings of His Divine Grace Śrīla B.R. Śrīdhar Mahārāj in this volume, *In the Light of Loving Devotion.*

Our approach in presenting this book is a little different from that of previous books of His Divine Grace, such as those so ably compiled by Śrīpād B.S. Goswāmī Mahārāj and others: *Search for Śrī Kṛṣṇa, Reality the Beautiful, Śrī Guru and His Grace, Golden Volcano of Divine Love*, and many more. Though the topics covered herein by Śrīla Śrīdhar Mahārāj are of eternal nature and value, it is nevertheless, from a relative viewpoint, now over thirty years since His Divine Grace withdrew in 1988 from amongst us to enter the eternal Pastimes of the Lord.

Thus newcomers to his teachings – whether through books, recorded talks and videos, or indeed the fortunate association with his dīkṣā (initiated) disciples who had direct association with His Divine Grace, especially the very embodiment of his mercy, Śrīla B.S. Govinda Mahārāj, his successor Sevāite-Āchārya, known affectionately as Śrīla Gurudev – these souls may be unfamiliar with Śrīla Śrīdhar Mahārāj's particular and unique way of presenting and explaining Kṛṣṇa consciousness. His delivery was always sweet in style and profound in content, emphasising the positive and progressive nature of true development in love for the Lord, and covering all important aspects of Vedic truth, including the divine Pastimes of Śrī Śrī Rādhā-Govinda, and Śrī Chaitanya Mahāprabhu; and this he did in a very careful and protective way, to avoid the pitfalls and misconceptions to which many seeking-souls, without expert guidance, may easily fall prey. While the text of this book, then, stands on its own by any criteria, we felt that for the newcomer to Śrīla Śrīdhar Mahārāj, or bhakti-yoga and Kṛṣṇa consciousness in general, some notations would be helpful. These references include for example, parallel thoughts on particular points to be found in other faith-traditions, and so on. These are given at the end of each chapter.

As the titles of the three parts of the book suggest, the talks follow a kind of progression which can be seen to fall roughly into the aspects of sambandha (relationship and environment); abhidheya (means to the end, devotional practice); and prayojana (the goal or destination – love of Kṛṣṇa) as delineated by the Rūpānuga Āchāryas. However due to the broad and comprehensive nature of Śrīla Śrīdhar Mahārāj's expression, in the text this division is by no means exclusive, and there is interpenetration, overlap, etc. Śrīla Śrīdhar Mahārāj's words proceeding from his high realisations, are, as so many have attested, ever fresh – they can be read repeatedly and deeper meanings will always reveal themselves. We pray, and we are sure, that sincerely seeking souls must benefit from them here.

All glories to Śrī Guru and Śrī Gaurāṅga

Part I

The Call of the Soul

from informal discourses
by
Śrīla Bhakti Rakṣak Śrīdhar
Dev-Goswāmī Mahārāj

With contemporary endnote explanations by
Śrī Bhakti Swarūp Tridaṇḍi Mahārāj

Chapter One

Soul-Gems

First Jewel: From Dream to Reality

Śrīla Śrīdhar Mahārāj: We are in the midst of a discordant element, a discordant atmosphere. We should try with proper adjustment to be a member of the world of harmony.
Student: Yes. We do not want another world war, we want only harmony…
Śrīla Śrīdhar Mahārāj: The world war will come and go. Creation and dissolution is everywhere, in small scale or bigger scale, it is the nature of this world of matter, but we should be properly adjusted. The whole world may vanish, and we may not be affected in any way.

Śukadev Goswāmī advises Parīkṣit Mahārāj, "Just kill your 'animal-consciousness' that you will die. You are not this body. Don't identify yourself with this material body. You are a subject, an onlooker. You are a seer, a feeler of this material creation. You are a separate entity – you are soul. When the body dies, you don't die, *na hanyate hanyamāne śarīre*, when the body is killed, the soul is not killed, he remains.[1] So, you must sever yourself from your body consciousness and seek your prospect in the higher sphere. Don't think that your prospect must be in this material world and that with the death of this material body, you will die. No." Even the atom bomb cannot do any harm to you:

> **nainaṁ chhindanti śastrāṇi**
> **nainaṁ dahati pāvakaḥ**[2]

"Weapons cannot pierce the soul and fire cannot burn it."

A Higher Existence

You are beyond the jurisdiction of any heinous activity of this mundane world. Nothing here can do any wrong to you; you exist above, by virtue of your very creation.

The threat of atomic war, that is, rather, a positive contribution – you will have to 'do or die!'[3] There is the physical civilisation, and the spiritual civilisation. Spiritual culture, civilisation, says, "Come hither – or be the victim of the atom bomb! Don't identify yourself with the physical body, for that is always in danger, wholesale, but try to get out of this physical existence, to attain some noble and higher existence for yourself. There is time yet. Whatever time is in your hand, utilise it to free yourself from your mal-identification that you will die by the atom-bomb. You won't die! If you can enter into Kṛṣṇa consciousness, there is no death. And not only no death, but there is a life of nectar, eternally.

"It is nearby, very close to you; but you have come here, you have run a long way to this material world – only to 'die'. But the nectar ocean of Kṛṣṇa consciousness is very near to you – as near to you as you are to yourself. Your real self is there. Why do you care for all these material things?"

The Deathless Self

At the conclusion of the *Śrīmad Bhāgavatam*, the warning is given to Parīkṣit Mahārāj – and to all of us – "This animal consciousness – butcher it! *Tvaṁ tu rājan mariṣyeti paśu-buddhim imāṁ jahi.*[4] Kill it, murder this animal consciousness about yourself, that you will die. Why have you allowed yourself to come down and identify yourself with this material world, which dies? You are above death, your real self is already above death. What you are, really, that is above death, and that does not die when the matter, your material body, is being transformed into so many constituents. This idea, that 'I shall die' – kill it, it is paśu-buddhi, animal consciousness. This false identification of your self with this body, is the cause of your material condition."

So, disconnect yourself from the material body, from body consciousness. Just as in a dream, you may see that your beheaded body is lying there – a beheaded man does not have any existence, any life, but in your dream you see that, and identify with it and suffer so much. All of what you are seeing now, it is like that, like a dream, but you are independent, as a 'seer' of this world. If the world is being destroyed, you are an onlooker, "O, the world is being destroyed." From aloof you are looking, you are not included there. You can make yourself separate from this mal-identification.

So, Śukadev Goswāmī tells Parīkṣit Mahārāj: "There is enough time. You do it! Immediately begin."[5]

Land of Infinite Prospect

You are an onlooker. You are a 'subject', not an 'object'. The objective world may vanish. The whole world, the entire solar system, may vanish, but you are not a member of that mortal world. You are a seer, always a seer, a subject. Your prospect is not with mortality, but is on the other side, the higher side, the super-subjective side. Don't mingle, entangle, yourself with this mortal world. You have come here to do that, for exploitation, but you are taṭastha, you are coming from the marginal plane, and on the other side of that plane is a land of prospect for you. It is infinitely spread there. So, begin your activity, your cultivation for such a land, and that will produce gems, gold, for you.

Endnotes to Chapter 1, First Jewel

1 **na jāyate mriyate vā kadāchin**
nāyaṁ bhūtvā bhavitā vā na bhūyaḥ
ajo nityaḥ śāśvato 'yaṁ purāṇo
na hanyate hanyamāne śarīre
(Śrīmad Bhagavad-gītā: 2:20)

"The soul is neither born nor dies; it has neither been, nor will be, 'created', because it is unborn and eternal. It is ever-youthful, and yet ancient. It is not destroyed when the body is destroyed."

2 **nainaṁ chhindanti śastrāṇi**
nainaṁ dahati pāvakaḥ
na chainaṁ kledayanty āpo
na śoṣayati mārutaḥ
(Śrīmad Bhagavad-gītā: 2:23)

"Weapons cannot pierce the soul and fire cannot burn it. Water cannot wet it, and air cannot dry it."

3 i.e. war can be a positive contribution, an impetus, a push to our spiritual endeavour and realisation. The soul does not die, so the expression that you will have to 'do or die' might appear

contradictory, but it is being used here in the sense of, "This is a great opportunity for you, the threat of impending atomic war. Now you will have to get yourself out of body-consciousness and into soul-consciousness and Kṛṣṇa consciousness – in short order!"

4 **tvaṁ tu rājan mariṣyeti paśu-buddhim imāṁ jahi**
na jātaḥ prāg abhūto 'dya deha-vat tvaṁ na naṅkṣyasi
(Śrīmad Bhāgavatam: 12.5.2)

"O King, give up the animalistic mentality of thinking, 'I am going to die.' Unlike the body, you have not taken birth. There was not a time in the past when you did not exist, and you are not about to be destroyed."

5 This advice can be found in Śukadev Goswāmī's initial answer to the question of Mahārāj Parīkṣit: "At this critical time, when I have only seven days to live, what is my duty? What should I do?" (Mahārāj Parīkṣit was confused by a variety of opinions and advice offered by sages of different schools of Vedic thought, and sought a definitive answer. When Śukadev Goswāmī, the great self-realised soul of whom most present in the assembly had heard by reputation, suddenly arrived at the meeting, they all deferred to him.) *Śrīmad Bhāgavatam,* Canto 2, Chapter 1.

Second Jewel: The Nature of the Soul

Question: Why is it that we are deceitful?
Śrī Śrīla Śrīdhar Mahārāj: The vulnerability, the weakness, imperfection, is within us, it is within our construction as soul. We are meagre, how can we be perfect? We have atomic existence, in every way. The atom cannot hold everything within itself. But adaptability – and so possibility, and prospect – that is also within us. Both aspects are there. The jīva is taṭasthā. It is a marginal point, endowed with the adaptability for two sides: he can come down to the material world, to exploit, and he can go up, to serve the higher. Association with the higher and association with the lower, these two, the double possibility is within him. He has such adaptability, and such is the constitution of all taṭasthā souls or jīvas, in their atomic existence. It is something inconceivable, but it has been explained in this way[1], ultimately. When argument is pushed to the limits of our understanding, we have to follow this way, this line of thought. We have to accept such 'beginning data'. We have to begin with data of such nature – both the innate vulnerability, and the adaptability, of the soul – then we can explain the possibilities of life, the different ways the soul may go.

Dynamic Character Within

Śrī Chaitanya Mahāprabhu says: *jīvera svarūpa haya Kṛṣṇera nitya-dāsa*[2] – the inner prospect of eternal service to Kṛṣṇa is there in the jīva, *Kṛṣṇera taṭasthā-śakti bhedābheda-prakāśa,* but he has come from, and he is found in, a particular potency of Kṛṣṇa, of the Absolute, which is taṭasthā.

'Taṭasthā' means, of a 'marginal' nature. That is, he is situated on the margin – on one side, the ocean of exploitation, and on the other, the ocean of dedication. The margin is of the nature of inertness, of indifference, but, closely inspected, we find there spiritual atoms that, though they apparently appear inert, indifferent, have within their inner constitution dynamic character. Such dynamic nature is there, though they are showing themselves as static outwardly. They may be taken into the dynamic position of exploitation, and it is also possible for them to participate in the dynamic plane of dedication. Their adaptability is such.[3]

Endnotes to Chapter 1, Second Jewel

[1] Explained in this way, that is, not by philosophical speculators but by the scriptures (Vedas, Purāṇas, etc.) and the bona fide saints, and Mahājans or authorities on devotional service.

[2] This śloka of *Śrī Chaitanya-charitāmṛta* is often given with its immediate next verse:

> **jīvera svarūpa haya kṛṣṇera 'nitya-dāsa'**
> **kṛṣṇera taṭasthā-śakti bhedābheda-prakāśa**
> **sūryāṁśa-kiraṇa, yaichhe agni-jvālā-chaya**
> **svābhāvika kṛṣṇera tina-prahāra śakti haya**
> *(Śrī Chaitanya-charitāmṛta: Madhya-līlā, 20.108–109)*

"It is the living entity's constitutional position to be an eternal servant of Kṛṣṇa because he is the marginal energy of Kṛṣṇa and a manifestation simultaneously one with and different from the Lord, like a molecular particle of sunshine or fire. Kṛṣṇa has three varieties of energy, of which the soul is one."

3 Śrīla Śrīdhar Mahārāj's explanation here is in answer to the initial question, "Why is it that we are deceitful?" Underlying this is the question of how can a 'pure' entity, the soul, take the wrong path? He is explaining the adaptability and vulnerability of the marginal soul and yet, as he says, there is an inconceivability about the nature of the soul itself – the principle of the jīva, jīva-tattva. Indeed, this should not be surprising since the soul is part of one of the energies of the Lord, and the Lord Himself is certainly inconceivable. Therefore, in *Bhagavad-gītā* after Kṛṣṇa explained in many verses to Arjuna the eternal nature of the soul, He concludes with this verse:

āścharya-vat paśyati kaśchid enam
āścharya-vad vadati tathaiva chānyaḥ
āścharya-vach chainam anyaḥ śṛṇoti
śrutvāpy enaṁ veda na chaiva kaśchit
(Śrīmad Bhagavad-gītā: 2.29)

"Some see the soul as astonishing, some describe it as astonishing, some hear of it as astonishing, while others though hearing of it, know nothing of it."

(Śrīla A.C. Bhaktivedānta Swāmī Prabhupāda gives the last line, *śrutvāpy enaṁ veda na chaiva kaśchit*, as: "Others, even after hearing about him, cannot understand him at all!")

Third Jewel: A Moment is Enough

Devotee: I think it will take a long time to attain Kṛṣṇa consciousness, in the full sense…
Śrīla Śrīdhar Mahārāj: It is not a question of time, but only earnestness is necessary. When Parīkṣit Mahārāj was appealing to Śukadev Goswāmī, "I have only seven days time, seven days to live before the brāhmaṇa's curse will take me away from this life," Śukadev replied: "This is enough time. Properly utilised, only a moment is sufficient."

kiṁ pramattasya bahubhiḥ
parokṣair hāyanair iha
varaṁ muhūrtaṁ viditaṁ
ghaṭate śreyase yataḥ
(*Śrīmad Bhāgavatam: 2.1.12*)

"What is the value of a prolonged life which is wasted, inexperienced by years in this world? Better a moment of full consciousness, because that gives one a start in searching after his supreme interest."

There are so many trees and so many mountains living for ages after ages, but what is the value of that? If properly utilised, one moment can make a revolutionary change within us towards the higher line of progress. The decision of a second, a moment, may help us greatly in our life, it may turn one's life around forever. Otherwise, if one is only sleeping[1] what is the benefit of living for ages and ages of time? One moment, if it is utilised for searching after truth – ātma-samīkṣā, self-analysis, "Who am I?" – that is the beginning of our eternal fortune. To enquire after our own self, "Who am I? Where am I at present, and what is my future prospect?" – our eternal fortune begins from here.

Universal Questions

So, Śukadev Goswāmī says: *kiṁ pramattasya bahubhiḥ parokṣair hāyanair iha varaṁ muhūrtaṁ viditaṁ,* years and years passed in unmindful[2] existence. A life unmindful of one's own interest, what is the good of that? But if even in a moment, you are conscious, you carefully utilise that time to find out your own solution, to become mindful of the solution of your life, to ask, "Who am I? Where am I and from where have I come? And what is my prospect?"

This tackling of the universal questions is the beginning, the start of your spiritual prospect. That searching tendency comes from sukṛti.[3] Then when such sukṛti is accumulated sufficiently, it becomes śraddhā, faith, and then Kṛṣṇa consciousness. But in the beginning there must be such self-analysis, self-enquiry – ātma-jijñāsā, brahma-jijñāsā – to want to know, to ask these questions, "Who am I, and what is my spiritual future?" With such self-analysis, your fortune begins. Then when one goes to look, and to compare, what should be your best prospect: Brahma consciousness, Paramātmā consciousness, Nārāyaṇa consciousness, then Kṛṣṇa consciousness – all these alternatives will come.

Endnotes to Chapter1, Third Jewel

1 'Sleeping' here of course, referring not literally to 'being asleep' (i.e. at night) but meaning existing in a state of unconsciousness, ignorant of one's spiritual purpose or goal in the human form of life.

Rocks, trees, etc. are generally existing in this state. In *Bhagavad-gītā*, Lord Kṛṣṇa when exhorting Arjuna to wake up to his duty as a warrior, to fight for dharma, at one point addresses him, "O Guḍākeśa, O Conqueror of sleep!"

In another verse (*Bhagavad-gītā: 2.69*) Kṛṣṇa says:

yā niśā sarva-bhūtānāṁ
tasyāṁ jāgarti saṁyamī
yasyāṁ jāgrati bhūtāni
sā niśā paśyato muneḥ

"What is night for all beings is the time of awakening for the self-controlled; and the time of awakening for all beings is night for the introspective sage."

2 'Mindful' and 'unmindful' of one's own existence – the term 'mindfulness' made popular especially from Buddhist texts on meditation has, in recent times, become a sound bite to supposedly validate any number of 'spiritual' paths or teachings.

Its secularised use in various forms of meditation has, however, been found effective in a psychological context in hospitals and prisons and for war veterans with post-traumatic stress disorder, etc. However, shorn of its real significance – to be mindful of one's own soul and of the Supersoul (God), as Śrīla Śrīdhar Mahārāj is using it here – mindfulness refers only to a concentrated impersonalistic awareness of 'everything in the field of consciousness' – to be 'in the moment', to be 'here now'. However, Śrīla Prabhupāda (Śrīla A.C. Bhaktivedānta Swāmī Prabhupāda) on one occasion is known to have pointedly said to a disciple who was thinking or acting in a 'spaced out' or unorganised way and even attempting to justify this by claiming it to be the result of their being absorbed in spiritual consciousness: "First become conscious then become Kṛṣṇa conscious!"

3 *Sukṛti*: auspicious spiritual fortune which manifests as the tendency for serious spiritual search. It is produced from the mercy

of the Lord received through the medium of service rendered to his agent, the devotee, initially done unknowingly (ajñāta-sukṛti), and later with knowledge/intent (jñāta-sukṛti). The mercy of the guru or devotee Vaiṣṇava (guru-kṛpā, Vaiṣṇava-kṛpā) is intimately related with the mercy of the Lord (Bhagavat-kṛpā).

Chapter Two

The Fields of Day and Night

Question: We have so many material desires, and the environment is also giving us some trouble, so sometimes we feel discouraged. How may we always maintain our enthusiasm and inspiration in spiritual life?

Śrīla Śrīdhar Mahārāj: If our desire for spiritual life is strong, then it may withstand so many oppositions from different conceptions, from different directions. There are so many things, desirable and undesirable. Sometimes we will be praised for our actions by a particular party, and sometimes there is some section that will discourage us, will abuse us. Everywhere this is the case, in whatever field of endeavour we work, such remarks of different types are sure to come. So here also, in the spiritual life, it is like that. Those who can appreciate the attempt will encourage us, and those who have no faith, they will discourage. It is quite natural.

So then, we have to rely on the appreciation of the Vaiṣṇava. *Vaiṣṇavī pratiṣṭhā, tāte kara niṣṭhā…*, the opinion of the devotee, that will have value for us. The worldly people, they do not have any appreciation for the high spiritual life, and they will naturally discourage: "What are they doing? They are wasting their life running after the 'will-o-the-wisp', after phantasmagoria." That will be their remark to us. "You are living in imagination! 'God' means only a kind of imagination, and leaving this world of reality you are running after that!"

The World of Soul

But the higher-standard people, the devotees, they know the value of sacrifice, sacrifice for the Absolute. They will think, to use the phrase of Hegel: that they must 'die to live'. You will have to dissolve your whole present ego that you are a 'master' and that you can do anything and everything. With such a wholesale 'death' you can peep into the other world of your soul. The Vaiṣṇavas will appreciate this, and avaiṣṇavas, the non-devotees, they will disparage. They will discourage and also cast so many bad names to us. But one who is awake, who understands, he is satisfied in himself and he won't care for these remarks, good or bad. He will think, "I can feel this, I can see with my inner eye that this is true, this is good, and I must march on in this line, march onward."

Such sincere seekers won't care for others' remarks – but they will have all regard for the remark of the Vaiṣṇavas, the devotees, that whether in their consideration I am good or bad. We shall give value to the appreciation or otherwise of the devotees, those who have taken their stand in spiritual truth, to their remark. If they say, "This is wrong" I shall be very careful to correct myself in that matter. We are concerned about the opinion of the expert in the spiritual department. The ordinary people's opinion has no value there. If the expert puts some remark about me, I must analyse what good or bad I am doing. I shall ask for his help and I shall correct myself. From purer to purer, I shall move ahead.

Darkness and Light

That should be our policy, *Vaiṣṇave-pratiṣṭhā*, the remark of the Vaiṣṇava will be of value to me, and not that of the ordinary people. Their opinion has no value because they are in darkness:

yā niśā sarva-bhūtānāṁ
tasyāṁ jāgarti saṁyamī
yasyāṁ jāgrati bhūtāni
sā niśā paśyato muneḥ
(Śrīmad Bhagavad-gītā: 2.69)

"That which is day for the self-controlled sage is night for all beings, and that which is day for all beings is night for the sage who sees."

The materialists are awake in a particular field, and the devotees are awake in another field, the spiritual field. There is the material field, the plane of exploitation; then the spiritual field, the plane of dedication; and the plane of renunciation – three planes of life. We want to enter the plane of dedication. Dedication also is of two kinds – one calculative, and the other is higher, it is of love and affection, 'blind love', and that is considered to be the highest.

Correct Yourself

The opinion of the spiritual guardians must have some value, and we shall try to follow that. If in their view of me, they see anything wrong, I shall try to give that up, to purge it out. In this way, *Vaiṣṇave-pratiṣṭhā*, what they want for me, I shall aspire for that, I shall try to become that. And the ordinary people, their remark has no value at all here.

gurur na sa syāt sva-jano na sa syāt
pitā na sa syāj jananī na sā syāt
daivaṁ na tat syāt na patiś cha sa syān
na mochayed yaḥ samupeta-mṛtyum
(Śrīmad Bhāgavatam: 5.5.18)

"One who cannot deliver his dependents from the path of repeated birth and death should never become a spiritual master, a father, a husband, a mother or a worshipable demigod."

We are always undergoing the mortal energy. We are a prey to that always. Who cannot relieve me from that general danger of life, he is not my own, and who can do so, he is my own. So if necessary I can leave everyone who is of such 'high order' related to me – my father, my mother, my so-called spiritual guide, my husband, my worshipable God, or demigod – all of them.[1]

Endnotes to Chapter 2

[1] This verse (*gurur na sa syāt...*) spoken by the incarnation of the Lord, Śrī Ṛṣabhadev, in instructing his sons, has been included by Śrīla Śrīdhar Mahārāj in his book *Śrī Śrī Prapanna-jīvanāmṛtam, 'Life-nectar of the Surrendered Souls (Positive and Progressive Immortality)'*, an anthology of verses from many Vaiṣṇava sources on the subject of surrender to the Lord, śaraṇāgati. One of the six limbs of that surrender is prātikūlya-vivarjanam or 'rejection of the unfavourable' (i.e. rejection of what is unfavourable for the service of the Lord). This verse appears there.

Introducing the verse by its essential meaning, Śrīla Śrīdhar Mahārāj writes: "When the traditional guru and guardians are found to be unfavourable, they too must surely be abandoned." His explanatory translation of the verse is given as follows: "One who cannot save other souls from the world of impending death – that is, one who cannot teach the path of devotion – he cannot be a teacher, although he may be called 'guru'; he cannot be a relative – he is not worthy of the designation; he cannot be a father – he is not qualified to beget a son; she cannot be a mother – she should not bear a child; he cannot be a god – the demigods who cannot deliver others from material bondage are not entitled to accept worship from human society; and he cannot be a husband – his hand is not fit to accept in marriage." *(Śrī Śrī Prapanna-jīvanāmṛtam, English edition, 1987, p.58)*

This is one out of many verses of *Śrīmad Bhāgavatam*, the 'spotless Purāṇa', which impress upon us unequivocally the extreme rarity, importance and value of the human birth in this world, and the seriousness with which it should be taken.

One is reminded of Śrī Kṛṣṇa's description of the process of Deity-worship (archanam) to Uddhava, His dear devotee, shortly before the Lord's leaving the material world along with the entire Yadu dynasty, just at the end of Dvāpara-yuga. After describing the process of worship, the Lord says one should finally stand before the Lord (the Deity) with folded hands and pray, "O Lord, please protect me. I am very fearful of this material existence, standing as I am within the mouth of death." (*Śrīmad Bhāgavatam,* 11th Canto.)

Chapter Three

The Vision of Faith

Lighthouses in the Ocean of Faith

Śrīla Śrīdhar Mahārāj: Though the Lord, the object of our heart's faith, is of infinite character, still some conceptions about Him have been given by the men of experience who are living in the ocean of faith. In that ocean many have their own experiences, and these have been recorded. Through their help we may approach Him. Like so many lighthouses, with their particular realisations they may help us, but that help must be bona fide and not mere concoction or imitation. Imitation is to take the experience of this world, these mortal things, and to thrust that into the world of faith. Such an anomaly is possible. So, very carefully and only through the line of the reliable sādhu, saint, we are to approach the higher realm. That is sādhu-saṅga.

We must be careful to know what are the qualifications of a sādhu. Their symptoms, as well as what should be the nature and the attitude of the enquirer, are given in the scripture. And faith – we must know how faith is to be real, and how faith is to work when we are in this material, 'unconscious', world. The most important thing we are to remember is that the object of our heart's faith, the Absolute, He is of subjective character – He can be kind to us, He can be affectionate to us, and He can guide us.

That the Lord can come to us, this is a very fundamental and substantial point to understand – the validity of the revealed truth[1] stands on this very foundation. It is not that only by some 'ascending' method we shall approach Him, but He can come down to our level and make Himself known to us. It is only through faith that we can come to this understanding that the transcendental substance, the object we are seeking through faith, He is endowed with all-power and all-consciousness and He is kind, benevolent and sweet. He is higher than us, infinitely higher, and our existence is infinitesimal, a much lower thing in comparison to Him. So our attitude towards Him should be of a corresponding nature.

A Real Transaction

What will be the real symptom of the enquirer, the disciple? Who is a real devotee, a seeker after truth? What is his qualification, his attitude, his nature? That is given in the scripture as well as the qualification of the guru, the guide.

tad viddhi praṇipātena paripraśnena sevayā
upadekṣyanti te jñānaṁ jñāninas tattva-darśinaḥ
(Śrīmad Bhagavad-gītā: 4.34)

"You will be able to attain knowledge by satisfying the divine master with submission, relevant enquiry and sincere service. The enlightened souls who are learned in scriptural knowledge and endowed with direct realisation of the Supreme Absolute Truth will impart divine knowledge to you."

So, the teacher, the master, must have both knowledge and realisation, and the student will be submissive, enquiring, and ready to render service, then the transaction between them will be bona fide. Otherwise, it will be a false transaction and that will not have any value, it will be a waste of energy.[2]

Faith does not allow us to believe that we are at liberty to think anything and everything – there is some guidance from above. The real transaction where that is possible will mean this, that guidance shall come from above.[3] So, the most essential thing, the very nature of śraddhā, faith, is that it is approaching towards the higher subject. In every way, it wants to approach Him, to approach that higher substance: sat, chit, ānanda – that is, in consideration of existence (sat), in consideration of knowledge (chit), and in consideration of affection and love (ānanda). These three points, three requirements as the goals of our existence, will be highly satisfied by the search through śraddhā, faith.

Faith and Experience

Faith always asks us to approach the higher, not the lower. "He, my guardian, is higher, is superior" – that is the basis of our faith. The scientist, the scientific brain, is always searching for some object which it can command and can utilise, but proper faith, śraddhā, is always connected with a substance which is higher in all respects than the searcher, the enquirer, himself. When the knowledge gained from experience stops, then faith arises. Experience, knowledge, is what we may acquire, and we are a subject in relation to it, but in relation to faith we are the object. When faith awakens, we shall try to understand that we are not subject, but object.

Proper guidance in faith is also necessary and that is given from the higher level. So, the nature of our enquiry, our search, will be as recommended in *Bhagavad-gītā* (4.34): with submission (praṇipāt), honest enquiry (paripraśna) and service (sevā). The *Upaniṣads* also tell us:

tad-vijñānārthaṁ sa gurum evābhigachchhet
samit-pāṇiḥ śrotriyaṁ brahma-niṣṭham
(Muṇḍaka Upaniṣad: 1.2.12)

"To understand these things properly, one must humbly approach, with firewood in hand, a spiritual master who is learned in the Vedas, and firmly devoted to the Absolute Truth."[4]

This is the general direction from the *Upaniṣads*.

And from *Śrīmad Bhāgavatam* (11.3.21):

tasmād guruṁ prapadyeta jijñāsuḥ śreya uttamam
śābde pare cha niṣṇātaṁ brahmaṇy upaśamāśrayam

"Therefore any person who seriously desires real happiness must seek a bona fide spiritual master and take shelter of him by initiation. The qualification of the bona fide guru is that he has realised the conclusions of the scriptures by deliberation and is able to convince others of these conclusions. Such great personalities, who have taken shelter of the Supreme Godhead leaving aside all material considerations, should be understood to be bona fide spiritual masters."

We should be very attentive to all these points; we should search ourselves, whether we are really approaching properly with real faith. Is it proper faith, or is it credulity? They are not the same. Is it real faith, or is our faith adulterated? We have to consider this. There are symptoms of real faith and we have to search these out for our guidance. This is extremely important.

Because we are dissatisfied with our present acquisition and we are taking a risk to jump towards a higher prospect, a higher way, so we must be very attentive that we are taking proper guidance as far as possible by us.

Faith and Reason

Though we are told that our present reasoning ability is not sufficient to take us up to our highest prospect, and that beyond our reason, śraddhā, faith is necessary, still as far as possible, we will utilise our reasoning and understanding in our search. When I first came to the mission, the Gauḍīya Maṭh, I heard from the devotees: *aprākṛta vastu nahe prākṛta-gochara*[5] – that the transcendental subject does not come within the grasp of material intelligence. I thought, "Yes, it is so, but still when I want to throw myself into this association, as far as possible I shall utilise my reasoning and intelligence to understand this very point because now I am going to jump into something which is beyond my control and calculation." So, to avoid misguidance, we must be particular to understand what is our reason, its limits, and what is śraddhā, faith.

Faith and Grace

Even if we are proceeding properly, there may be some obstacle in the way. Some unknown hindrance may come to trouble us and delay our advancement, but still we will do our best to always carefully maintain our faith. We may see that there are many around us, of our own group, who are falling while attempting to approach the same goal. Some are falling down next to us, but we must continue to stand. When we are proceeding in an organised way, in an association, many things are possible: some are standing, some falling down, others taking rest or falling back, and some are leaving the campaign altogether. So many things are occurring around us, but still we should go forward. And for that, what will be our capital? How will I go forward, when I find that so many cannot? That is depending on our faith. We will have to collect so much faith and so much goodwill, and that is our capital: "Many of us began together on this path of advancement, and now so many are going back, but I shall have to go ahead, I shall have to consolidate and strengthen my energy and go forward – alone if necessary." Our faith should be so strong, so solid and substantial. "Alone I shall go. Whatever difficulties I may find on my way, I must cross over them, by the grace of my Lord."

In this way we must make ourselves fit, fit for exclusive devotion. And we must always try to find good association. But sometimes it may be that there is no association and we are alone – still, we must go ahead, and at that time the 'beacon lights', the great devotees, they are indispensable for us.[6]

The Dynamic of Progress

Always we will try to find out higher association. Progress means to eliminate something and to accept another, so we must be alert to see that there are so many others who can help my progress in life. With this eye open we shall go forward.

In the śāstra so many levels are shown to us – the conceptions about the Lord from Chatuḥsana (the four Kumāras), from Brahmā, from Śiva, from Śrī (Lakṣmī) – and by elimination we are to understand who among them is superior to all. By elimination, the gradation, the progression, is shown.

karmibhyaḥ parito hareḥ priyatayā vyaktiṁ yayur jñāninas
tebhyo jñāna-vimukta-bhakti-paramāḥ premaika-niṣṭhās tataḥ
(Upadeśāmṛta: verse 10)

"In the śāstra it is said that of all types of fruitive workers, he who is advanced in knowledge of the higher values of life is favoured by the Supreme Lord with devotional service. He is superior to the others. However, one who has actually attained prema, pure love of Kṛṣṇa, is superior to him."

In the discussion between Rāmānanda Rāya and Śrī Chaitanya Mahāprabhu (*Śrī Chaitanya-charitāmṛta: Madhya-līlā, Chapter 8*), Rāmānanda was describing progressively higher stages of bhakti, and Mahāprabhu at each stage said, "*eho bāhya, āge kaha āra*": "Go further – go deeper, go higher." But some go to a particular stage, and there they stop.

It is shown in the *Bṛhat-Bhāgavatāmṛtam* of Śrīla Sanātan Goswāmī how the cowherd-boy Gopa Kumār, beginning from the lowest stage, is gradually making progress through different levels, and at last is coming to the Kṛṣṇa conception in the friendly relationship, sakhya-rasa. It is described there how he is progressing stage by stage, through elimination and new acceptance, from one level up to the next. Each time, at first, his new association seems to be very helpful, but gradually that company seems to him to be stale, then through some agent of the higher plane, a chance is given to him. Leaving his present position, Gopa Kumār is going with him to that higher plane. In this way, his progress, through faith and with the help of so many others, is shown.

Just as in this tangible world, there are so many planes, like that of the sun, moon, the earth and so on, so in the plane of faith there are so many levels, and by the process of elimination there is progress. This is described in the scriptures, and we have to study it and take the benefit. Whenever there is any doubt, we shall consult with the higher agent, devotee, and so make progress.

The Heart's Demand (1)

The general understanding of our existence and prospect is *sat-chit-ānanda* – existence, knowledge and happiness, fulfilment. Mere existence (sat) cannot fulfil our inner hankering, also knowledge or consciousness (chit) cannot do so, but rasa, taste, ānandam – that is our fulfilment. That rasa is also of different types. This is the main conception we are to understand. We have to seek our own prospect by properly differentiating, and so always improve. We will be always wakeful, and conscious about the environment. Our sacrificing spirit must increase, we must go deeper. We must dive deep into that service spirit, and we must kill our false ego, our separate interest, in order to live in the plane of service.

We must 'die to live' – and in that death also, there is gradation: deep, deeper, deepest. Through elimination and new acceptance there is gradation, and progress.

Kṛṣṇa says, *sarva-dharmān parityajya Mām ekaṁ śaraṇaṁ vraja (Śrīmad Bhagavad-gītā: 18.66).* "Give up all kinds of religion and surrender to Me alone."

So the duties we find ourselves in the midst of, may be left for the acceptance of higher duties. In this way we are to make progress.

The Heart's Demand (2)

We will always consult the sādhu, the devotee, and the śāstra, scripture. They will guide us in the ocean of faith towards what to us at present is unknown and unknowable but which is known and knowable to a certain section. They have given direction to us, and we shall take advantage of that help. In this way, by the help of saints and scriptures we shall improve our fortune.

We are to eliminate the mortal, transient things, and realise our eternal existence, that is, 'sat'; we shall satisfy our reason, 'chit'; and then we shall satisfy our heart, 'ānandam'. Śrī Chaitanya Mahāprabhu says that the demand of our heart is the primary necessity in us. We shall follow the direction of that heart's demand, and that will give us the highest fulfilment – not the satisfaction of our reason, our knowledge, or to have only eternal existence. Eternal existence has no meaning if it is not conscious of itself. Consciousness also has no meaning if it does not give fulfilment. So, considering this truth, we shall go on, further and further, to a higher life.

Hṛdayena-abhyanujñāto, our own heart will be our witness; we shall feel within our heart whether we are loser or gainer. Such possibility is there because that 'tasting machine' is within us.

Śrīmad Bhāgavatam says,

bhidyate hṛdaya-granthiś chhidyante sarva-saṁśayāḥ
kṣīyante chāsya karmāṇi dṛṣṭa evātmanīśvare *(2.21)*[7]

Bhidyate hṛdaya-granthi – once the knot of attachment in the heart has been dissolved, our karma, our connection with this material world, will evaporate and a spacious knowledge will come to satisfy us. Then we shall feel, we shall be able to trace, the object of our life – love for the Lord – everywhere. We shall feel it: *dṛṣṭa evatmanīśvare*, His love has embraced us from all sides, it is sympathetic to us, helping us from every side. That is the awakening of our heart, and that is home. Home is where the heart is, and we shall feel home comfort there.

So, we must go back to God, back to home. Home means where everyone is loving me and they are caring for my interest. They are having my interest at heart. I may be careless about my own interest, but the whole environment there is so favourable towards me, so affectionate, and so useful, and helpful – I cannot even estimate it, just as the child cannot have any estimation about its mother's affection. But there we find home comfort and motherly affection, and all are friends around me and they are seeing to my interest. I may not find, or may not know, my own interest, but they are alert, always alert for my welfare.

Endnotes to Chapter 3

1 Revealed truth: Vedic truth, the divine-sound, spiritual revelation which 'descends' (avaroha-panthā) from the spiritual realm beyond human intellect. This knowledge was originally imparted from Kṛṣṇa Himself to Prajāpati Brahmā, then orally from Brahmā to his disciples, and from them to theirs, in disciplic succession. It is also called the śruti, 'knowledge which is heard'. At the beginning of the present world, the present age, kali-yuga, it was put into writing by the sage Dvaipāyana Vedavyāsa, in the form of the Vedas and their corollaries.

2 The importance of accepting a master for spiritual advancement in life cannot be overstated. It is the first of the sixty-four items in devotional service to Śrī Śrī Rādhā Kṛṣṇa mentioned by Śrīla Rūpa Goswāmī, the leader of the followers of Lord Chaitanya Mahāprabhu. (The Gauḍīya Vaiṣṇavas are known as Rūpānugas, the followers of Śrī Rūpa.) To discuss this subject of Guru-tattva in any depth, would require a separate treatment; however, though in

varying levels of depth and detail, a similar principle exists in all genuine faith traditions. The Carmelite theologian and mystic, St. John of the Cross, in reply to those who asked whether a soul could make progress without the guidance of a spiritual master, declared simply, "The soul which has virtue but remains on its own without a master is like a burning coal which is left to itself; it loses its glow and grows cold."

3 It is indeed the case that reason and intellect cannot reach to, or experience, the Infinite Absolute, being themselves of material nature, part of the manifestation of the material energy – as *Bhagavad-gītā* (7.4) says: the 'separated energy' of the Lord. But faith can do so, that is, it can connect, it can make the direct connection between the soul and God. Desire, will, intention, and love, with faith as their foundation, is the channel through which the soul can experience the Lord, and, in the higher stages, even attract Him to her.

The English poet, novelist, and scholar Evelyn Underhill (see Note 1) wrote: "Where the office of thought ends, there the office of will and feeling begins."

"Where intellect must stay without," says Ruysbroeck (see Note 2) "these may enter in." Desire and intention are the most dynamic of our faculties … they are the true explorers of the Infinite, the instruments of our ascent to God. Reason comes to the foot of the mountain; it is the industrious will urged by the passionate heart which climbs the slope." (From *The Essentials of Mysticism*, Oneworld Publications, 1999, p.83).

This is all good. And yet – and this may appear paradoxical, even contradictory, but it is stressed in this chapter by Śrīla Śrīdhar Mahārāj, and spiritual seekers ignore it at their peril, many a one has lost their way by doing so – faith requires guidance.

Saint Augustine wrote: *fides instructionem desiderat*, 'faith desires instruction'. Just as conscience alone is not sufficient without assistance, because alone it can lead into the cul-de-sac of relativism where no absolute values exist, only "my conscience tells me to do such-and-such…", conscience, like faith, must be 'informed' – guided by scripture, knowledge, and spiritual tradition.

In this way, faith must be real, and not imaginary or theoretical, or mere 'credulity' as Śrīla Śrīdhar Mahārāj says. Michael Casey OCSO, Cistertian monk and spiritual mentor, puts it well when he writes: "Faith is the origin and ongoing engine of all spiritual life. It is God's gratuitous gift to us, but to produce its fruits it calls for a response. We are obliged to render what St. Paul calls "the obedience of faith" (*Rom.* 1:5; 16:26). This obedience leads to the works of faith about which the *Epistle of James* writes: "What profit is there, my brothers, if someone claims to have faith but has no works? Is such a faith able to save? Faith by itself, if it has no works, is dead… You see that a person is justified by works and not by faith alone… Just as the body without the spirit is dead, so faith without works is dead." (*Jas.* 2:14,17,24,26).

As Śrīla Śrīdhar Mahārāj says about surrender to the Lord, that it is not merely a 'state-of-being' but is a force, dynamic and progressive, so it is with faith. Casey again: "Faith, although interior, is living and active. It cannot be without impact on how we experience life or how we respond to its opportunities and challenges. It is in responding to the gift of faith that we open our lives to God. Faith is our connection to God. The first and fundamental work of faith is to actualise that connection…" (from *Grace: On the Journey to God,* p.128).

The progressive movement of surrender, through faith, and how it manifests in service to the Lord at its different stages of development, is beautifully brought out in the Vaiṣṇava teachings in the talk between Śrī Chaitanya Mahāprabhu and Rāmānanda Rāya as recorded in *Śrī Chaitanya-charitāmṛta,* Madhya-līlā, Chapter 8). There, in the course of his outline of the ontological development of Kṛṣṇa consciousness, and how the living entity is best to serve Kṛṣṇa, Rāmānanda quoted *Bhagavad-gītā,* 18.66: *sarva-dharmān parityajya*

Mām ekaṁ śaraṇam vraja.... Kṛṣṇa appeals to Arjuna "Give up all dharmas and surrender to Me alone..." This verse, which is generally understood by scriptural commentators as the 'last word' of *Śrī Gītā*, and as representing the acme of bhakti, devotion, was actually rejected by Śrī Chaitanyadev as being such – for, while in it the Lord asks for surrender, there is no indication here as to service, or the form which the actual service of a soul surrendered to the Lord will take thereafter. Śrī Chaitanya Mahāprabhu therefore said to Rāmānanda: *eho bāhya, āge kaha āra*: "Go further..."; that is, "Say something more, something better..."

4 The expression 'with firewood in hand' refers to the wood which is to be used in the fire sacrifice which is the sacramental ritual traditionally conducted at the time of the disciple's spiritual initiation. This will be collected by the disciple himself, it is not that his guru will supply it. The meaning, in other words, is as Śrīla Śrīdhar Mahārāj has elsewhere explained that the disciple is not coming to demand, or to try to 'extract', anything from the spiritual master – he is coming of his own free heart and will, without any hidden agenda, to surrender, to enquire, and to render service. He will come "bringing his own bed and baggage".

5 **aprākṛta vastu nahe prākṛta-gochara**
veda-purāṇete ei kahe nirantara
(Śrī Chaitanya-charitāmṛta: Madhya-līlā, 9.194)

"Spiritual substance is never within the jurisdiction of the material conception. This is always the verdict of the Vedas and Purāṇas."

6 When there is sometimes no association of a living sādhu available, the exemplary lives and teachings of great devotees of the lineage are there to follow, as 'beacon lights'.

7 "Thus the knot in the heart is pierced, and all misgivings are cut to pieces. The chain of fruitive activities is terminated when one sees the self as master."

Note 1: Evelyn Underhill (1875–1941), an Anglo-Catholic writer and spiritual seeker who practised, studied and wrote about prayer, especially its meditational and contemplative dimensions, and the stages of development therein. Her book *Mysticism* has been influential among Western thinkers in this field since its publication in 1911.

Note 2: Jan van Ruysbroeck (1293–1381) was one of the 'Rhineland mystics' along with Meister Eckhart, Johann Tauler and Henry Suso. He is generally acknowledged as the greatest Flemish contemplative and wrote several books, most famously *The Adornment of the Spiritual Marriage*. Underhill quotes him frequently in her writing.

Chapter Four

The Charm of the Upper World

A Life Worth Living

In the divine realm, in the abode of the Lord, Kṛṣṇa, we will not be a master – rather, we shall be very eager to consider ourselves to be a slave – that realm is so high. There is a competition in the conception of slavery, to be the slave of a slave of the slave of the Lord! If we have enough boldness to sacrifice ourselves to the extreme, then we can hope to live in that domain. Hegel expressed, 'die to live'. The conception underlying this is very broad, bold and of very deep meaning.

The scriptures and the saints ask, "Are you ready to die to your self? Then we can recommend a land where you can live." But are you bold enough to 'die'? That there is nothing worth living for in this plane of māyā, illusion – are you ready to come to this conclusion? That every particle here is worthless, and also mischievous,[1] have you come to realise that? If you think that this world is not worth living in at all, then you will be easily ready to 'die' wholesale, and you will be given the opportunity of living a proper life, after death. That is really, 'life after death'.[2]

So, you are to 'die to live'. And Kṛṣṇa, He is for Himself, and not for any 'ghost' like you![3] He is for Himself, and He is so dignified, and everyone, every atom, of His plane, is so dignified, they should all be regarded with honour. Everything there, the very soil there, is such. Do you like to live in that land, to become a slave there?

Paradise Lost

In John Milton's poem *Paradise Lost* is just the opposite statement: "It is better to reign in hell, than to serve in heaven." That is Satan's opinion, but really the truth is the contrary: it is better to serve in heaven, than to reign in hell. The satanic doctrine was the cause of the fall. Paradise was lost because Adam and Eve lost their faith in śaraṇāgati, in surrender. Their faith in the truth of surrender was disturbed, and they came to live according to their own free will and judgement, under their own responsibility, and so they had to come down into the world of calculation, to 'earn and eat', to 'labour and live'. In Paradise, without labour, sustenance used to come. When Adam and Eve were in a surrendered position no labour was necessary, but automatically everything was provided for them.

The soul does not require any food to maintain a material body. It has its spiritual, eternal body, and there is no need of any addition, of anything from the outside, to keep up its vitality. That is the pure, surrendered, spiritual life – the world of the soul. But when Adam and Eve came to misuse their free-choice, instead of that, their life became 'labour and live'. That entered the world, and Satan was at the back of this. He tempted them: "Why are you a slave? There is the tree of knowledge. Take from that!"

Temptation of Knowledge

We souls in the world are very much enamoured by knowledge, but *Śrīmad Bhāgavatam* has said "Don't rely on your knowledge." The fruit of the Tree of Knowledge was tasted by first Eve then Adam, and that 'Tree of Knowledge' is dangerous, it brought them down here, down to the world of calculation.

The world of surrender is the society of the good, the higher society where there is no hypocrisy and no conspiracy. So, knowledge – calculation of what is 'good', what is 'bad' – this is meaningless there. Instead, there is an automatic flow of goodness in the whole atmosphere. There is no doubt, no suspicion, and no meanness to cheat one another, so there is no question of any 'calculation'. That is so in the lower part of the spiritual abode, in Vaikuṇṭha, and higher again in Goloka it is more beautiful, more loving, more sustaining, more sweet, and more ecstatic.

A Sweet Home

What is necessary for us is practical faith in that sort of life, in the charm of that sort of life. And Kṛṣṇa promises,

sarva-dharmān parityajya
mām ekaṁ śaraṇaṁ vraja
ahaṁ tvāṁ sarva-pāpebhyo
mokṣayiṣyāmi mā śuchaḥ
(Śrīmad Bhagavad-gītā: 18.66)

"Give up all kinds of religion and surrender unto Me alone. I will liberate you from all sins, do not despair."

In the Bible, there is a history of the soul's fall, but there it is not described very clearly or minutely how the soul is going up towards the Lord. It is vague – only that the Son of God has come to take the soul up to the divine abode, the abode of God. The fall of Adam and Eve, how that came about, that is very clear, but how the soul is taken from this plane to that, from the lower to the higher, there is not any clear or explicit description, nor of who are residing there in that higher plane. There are so many 'Christ-like' souls who have full faith in God's land, God's actions, God's goodness, so much so that they treat all the wealth, the prosperity, the charm of this world of enjoyment as nothing. They will 'trample it under their feet'[4]. They have died to this world: "I resign all covetable posts in this world, however great – of kingship, leadership, or of the charm of a lover like Romeo, or a beloved like Juliet – all dismissed. I am ready to dismiss all these things for a higher life, a life mystic, unknown, a sweet, sweet life, a sweet home."

Life, the Afterlife – and Beyond

Bhagat Singh was one of the leading anarchists in Punjab, and he was captured and given capital punishment, a death sentence. One gentleman asked him, "The day of your death is drawing near – how do you feel?" He replied, "I am very eager to see the afterlife. This life is finished for me, completely. I have no charm for this life – now I am very eager to see the afterlife."

But Bhagat Singh did not know that his afterlife must be also similar to this! The anarchist's afterlife, what kind of good can it be? He has attraction for this mundane world, and he cannot tolerate another's 'ownership' here and he wants to snatch the ownership of this material world from him. So, what kind of afterlife he will see, will it be anything very glorious?

But we are to see, rather, all achievements, all positions in this world, neglectfully, as of no importance, no dignity – even the post of the creator of this material world, Brahmā. He is its creator and master, but he is himself within the relativity of this world, which is mortal and nasty. His position is also condemnable, what to speak of ordinary persons like us. When even the creator of this whole mundane world is also surrounded by inauspicious, reactionary consequences of mortal life, then what is our position? It is so meagre.

karmaṇāṁ pariṇāmitvād
ā-viriñchyād amaṅgalam
vipaśchin naśvaraṁ paśyed
adṛṣṭam api dṛṣṭa-vat
(Śrīmad Bhāgavatam: 11.19.18) [5]

"An intelligent person should see that any material activity is subject to constant transformation, and that even on the planet of Lord Brahmā there is thus simply unhappiness. Indeed, a wise man can understand that just as all that he has seen is temporary, similarly, all things within the universe have a beginning and an end."

Above Brahmā, is Śiva. His position is that of the liberated soul. The temperament of the liberated soul in that plane is, *śivo 'ham, śivo 'ham, śivo 'ham*, "I am independent, I do not care for material comfort. Independent of that, as soul, I can live. I don't care for any comfort, acquisition, or achievement – I am sufficient in myself. I am self-sufficient, ātmarāma. I don't require any exploitation of this world nor of anyone."

That plane is spiritual, but it is the marginal position, just on the border of the higher realm. Above that plane is another domain and it is so high and so charming, that when the soul comes into contact with it, it feels, "O, I want to enter as a slave into this holy and magnanimous land." He wants to be a member of that land, even the lowest member. He will feel even an ant's position in that noble domain is something to be envied. That realm is Vaikuṇṭha.

Again, over Vaikuṇṭha is Goloka, the most comprehensive and most subtle, all-pervading plane. It is the highest plane to be found in all of existence – the foundation of all different varieties of planes of experience. Goloka is all beauty and love. Beauty and love are of similar nature. That plane is beyond power, power-seeking – it is all-sweet.

The Gift of Vedavyāsa

This conception has been definitely brought down from the highest plane for us by Mahāprabhu and Nityānanda and by *Śrīmad Bhāgavatam*, the last gift of Vedavyāsa. Revealed truth in its greatest form and magnitude, was given by Vyāsadev here in India, from Badarikāśram. The key to that treasure-chest was given first to his son, Śukadev. Śukadev tried to impress the then scholars of India with that highest ideal of the whole theological world, and did so, successfully, with his delivery to Mahārāj Parīkṣit at Sukartala. After that, was a second sitting at Naimiṣāraṇya where sixty thousand brāhmaṇa scholars met together just before the onset of this 'iron-age', kali-yuga.

At that gathering was one special scholar who had been present at the assembly of Śukadev Goswāmī. He was an extraordinary scholar, śruti-dhara – that is, by hearing once, he can remember the subject forever. His name was Sūta Goswāmī, or Ugraśravā, meaning 'one whose aural reception is of the highest degree, is extraordinary'. And at Naimiṣāraṇya, Sūta Goswāmī distributed that knowledge, the *Bhāgavata*, to the scholars there. So, there were four sittings, in all: the first from

Nārada to Vyāsadev, second from Vyāsa to Śukadev, third from Śuka to Parīkṣit in the assembly of sages at Sukartala, and the fourth at Naimiṣāraṇya from Ugraśravā Sūta to Śaunaka and the ṛṣis. Then Vyāsadev wrote three introductory verses, and with that, the whole composition was distributed to the world.

Beyond Jealousy

The three poems which Vyāsadev wrote are:

janmādy asya yato 'nvayād itarataś chārtheṣv abhijñaḥ svarāṭ
tene brahma hṛdā ya ādi-kavaye muhyanti yat sūrayaḥ
tejo-vāri-mṛdāṁ yathā vinimayo yatra tri-sargo 'mṛṣā
dhāmnā svena sadā nirasta-kuhakaṁ satyaṁ paraṁ dhīmahi
(Śrīmad Bhāgavatam: 1.1.1)

dharmaḥ projjhita-kaitavo 'tra paramo nirmatsarāṇāṁ satāṁ
vedyaṁ vāstavam atra vastu śivadaṁ tāpa-trayonmūlanam
śrīmad-bhāgavate mahā-muni-kṛte kiṁ vā parair īśvaraḥ
sadyo hṛdy avarudhyate 'tra kṛtibhiḥ śuśrūṣubhis tat-kṣaṇāt
(Śrīmad Bhāgavatam: 1.1.2)

then:

nigama-kalpa-taror galitaṁ phalaṁ
śuka-mukhād amṛta-drava-saṁyutam
pibata bhāgavataṁ rasam ālayam
muhur aho rasikā bhuvi bhāvukāḥ
(Śrīmad Bhāgavatam: 1.1.3)

These verses represent sambandha (relationship), abhidheya (means), prayojana (end). First is sambandha, the proper understanding of our own self and the environment. The second is the means to the end, and the third, the proper conception of the ultimate goal of life, the destination, different from all other recommendations given in various theological scriptures.[6]

This is the speciality of this book, the *Bhāgavatam*: after liberation, how one can live a dignified life. And it is meant for those who are *nirmatsarāṇāṁ satāṁ*, free from all jealousy. Vyāsadev states in the very beginning that it is meant for those saints who are nirmatsara, completely free from any trace of jealousy. 'Jealousy' means, one is unable to tolerate anyone higher than oneself. That is the test. At every step you are to feel, without prejudice, that everything, all the paraphernalia surrounding you, is holding a higher position than yourself. If you are jealous, you won't be able to advance a single step here in the conception Vyāsadev is giving. Only if jealousy is fully eliminated in you – if you are ready to tolerate that everyone you come across is holding a higher position than yourself and you do not mind it, you do not feel any disturbance from that, it produces no reaction in you – if you feel that every atom of dust in the higher plane is holding a superior position to you, and you are the slave there, if you can accommodate yourself in such a way, then you will have a higher place where you can enter, and live.

Not A Luxury

So, the *Bhāgavatam* is not for any ordinary saint. Vyāsadev says, "*nirmatsarāṇāṁ satāṁ* – jealousy must be totally eliminated in you, then you can hope to come, to study and to be able to understand what I say: that everything is superior to you, and you are the lowest. You must have that temperament. It is the minimum demand from you, and to satisfy that demand will fulfil everything, complete everything, and then you can be free, you can make free progress and freely live and move there in that domain." This is the death sentence to the claims of the sahajiyā class of thinkers. Because the substance of the very elements in Vaikuṇṭha is superior to you, it is all chinmaya, spiritual.

vaikuṇṭhera pṛthivy-ādi sakala chinmaya
māyika bhūtera tathi janma nāhi haya
(Śrī Chaitanya-charitāmṛta: Ādi-līlā, 5.53)

"The earth, water, fire, air, and ether of Vaikuṇṭha are all spiritual. Material elements are not found there."

What to speak of Goloka, the topmost plane, in the lower hemisphere of the spiritual world also, in Vaikuṇṭha, everything is made of spiritual substance. Every atom there is spiritual, and it is of higher quality than you yourself, the soul, who wants to enter there. So, to want to enter into that domain, and have the company of the Nārāyaṇa-bhaktas, the devotees of Lord Nārāyaṇa, and then higher still, the association of devotees in Goloka Vṛndāvan, it is not a light matter or a luxury, it is not something so easy. Without first deserving it, you cannot have it. But 'sahajiyā' – that is only to imitate here in the plane of flesh and blood. The sahajiyās, they are plodding in the mud of materialism, and thinking they are in the divine lake of Rādhā Kuṇḍa.

Endnotes to Chapter 4

1 'Worthless', when not seen and understood as Lord Kṛṣṇa's energy, and so not utilised in His service. In this way, the material world is 'mischievous' to the soul, simply diverting it from Kṛṣṇa consciousness.

2 Real 'life after death' is life with a purpose, that of serving Kṛṣṇa, and not merely a 'positive' answer to the general question "Is there life after death?" i.e. "Does the soul continue to exist after death?"

3 They are 'ghost-like' in the sense that the soul, coming from the taṭasthā plane, the marginal energy of the Lord, though pure spirit, is of an intrinsically vulnerable nature, and so subject to mistakes, illusion, etc., hence their present conditioned state in the material world. In this way they are, as it were, ephemeral, or 'ghost-like', in comparison with the position and nature of the Supreme Lord Kṛṣṇa, the inviolate, unconditioned, ever-playful Absolute Truth. ('Ghost-like' also, perhaps, because ghosts are well known for their tendency to disturb others!)

4 It would seem consistent with the foregoing narrative, that the 'Christ-like souls' to whom Śrīla Śrīdhar Mahārāj is referring, are those souls who after death in this world have "gone up from this plane to that" and are now "residing there, in that higher plane", in the spiritual world. However, it also refers to souls of high purity and realisation still embodied on earth, because he goes on to say that they "treat all the charm of this world of enjoyment as nothing." Certainly this is not inconsistent with the Vaiṣṇava-siddhānta that a soul can be 'Christ-like', in any condition – materially embodied or otherwise. It is a question of their state of consciousness.

5 This verse is from the *Uddhava-gītā*, Kṛṣṇa's teachings to His dear devotee Uddhava, as recorded in *Śrīmad Bhāgavatam,* 11th canto. Kṛṣṇa is here reiterating the teachings on dharma which Bhīṣmadev at the Battle of Kurukṣetra, on his 'bed of arrows' waiting to depart this world, imparted to Mahārāj Yudhiṣṭhir who was about to take the throne as world Emperor.

(Grandfather Bhīṣma, though fated to support the miscreant Duryodhana in his war against the Pāṇḍavas, was a great devotee of Kṛṣṇa and was happy to receive his death at the hands of Kṛṣṇa and Arjuna. He is also one of the twelve Mahājanas, or famous authorities on devotional service.)

6 The translations of these three verses from *Śrīmad Bhāgavatam* are given as follows:

1.1.1: "O my Lord, Śrī Kṛṣṇa, son of Vasudev, O all-pervading Personality of Godhead, I offer my respectful obeisances unto You. I meditate upon Lord Śrī Kṛṣṇa because He is the Absolute Truth and the primeval cause of all causes of the creation, sustenance and destruction of the manifested universes. He is directly and indirectly conscious of all manifestations, and He is independent because there is no other cause beyond Him. It is He only who first imparted the Vedic knowledge unto the heart of Brahmājī, the original living being. By Him even the great sages and demigods are placed into illusion, as one is bewildered by the illusory representations of water seen in fire, or land seen on water. Only because of Him do the material universes, temporarily manifested by the reactions of the three modes of nature, appear factual, although they are unreal. I therefore meditate upon Him, Lord Śrī Kṛṣṇa, who is eternally existent in the transcendental abode, which is forever free from the illusory representations of the material world. I meditate upon Him, for He is the Absolute Truth."

1.1.2: "Completely rejecting all religious activities which are materially motivated, this *Bhāgavata Purāṇa* propounds the highest truth, which is understandable by those devotees who are fully pure in heart. The highest truth is reality distinguished from illusion for the welfare of all. Such truth uproots the threefold miseries. This beautiful *Bhāgavatam*, compiled by the great sage Vyāsadev [in his maturity], is sufficient in itself for God realisation. What is the need of any other scripture? As soon as one attentively and submissively hears the message of *Bhāgavatam*, by this culture of knowledge the Supreme Lord is established within his heart."

1.1.3: "O expert and thoughtful men, relish *Śrīmad-Bhāgavatam*, the mature fruit of the desire tree of Vedic literatures. It emanated from the lips of Śrī Śukadev Goswāmī. Therefore this fruit has become even more tasteful, although its nectarean juice was already relishable for all, including liberated souls."

Chapter Five

The Infinite Embrace

Happy Association

Surrender to the Lord, that means 'die to live'. And death's jurisdiction is so wide – not only physical death but death of all our ambitions, our ambitious aspirations. And then, to live – and living in that divine realm is so great, so wonderful. It is an unknown, strange thing, in comparison to our present living. But that is really living, among all who are good, all high, all divine, and all superior to us. How happy is that living, that life! Wherever I am moving and breathing there, everything is of higher quality than my own self – how happy it is, how elevated and elevating! But do we have such courage to live there? To die a wholesale death to all of our experience, to be severed from all the valuable things we have ever gathered experience of – is that possible for us? It is not so easy, that all the ideals that we have ever accumulated or come into association with, all are to be given up. Not only physical acquisitions, but all our mental acquisitions and prospects, all are to be discarded. There must be a wholesale dissolution of mind and body, and only the naked soul is to be taken to that land where are living so many saints of that highest calibre. That is the Reality, and it is stranger than a dream, stranger than fiction to us at present. The standard of our prospect should be raised so high.

Standard of Sacrifice

What is the meaning of self-abnegation? If we can have some conception of the truth, then we shall see that what we are aspiring for at present is all nasty, all sinful. Why should I be master of so many things? Why? We hate slavery, but if we have some conception of the truth we will be able to understand how dignified it is to have the position of a slave to such wonderful goodness, such a wonderful master. And it is not impossible to peep into that higher position of truth. We will be eager to cast ourselves at the feet of those holy persons who bring us news from that land.

Once in Purī, Mahāprabhu told to Sanātan Goswāmī:

sanātana, deha-tyāge kṛṣṇa yadi pāiye
koṭi-deha kṣaṇeke tabe chhāḍite pāriye
(Śrī Chaitanya-charitāmṛta: Antya-līlā, 4.55)

"Sanātan, if it would have been possible that by giving up this body I could get Kṛṣṇa, then in a moment I am ready to sacrifice this body, I am ready to invite death, bodily death, crores of times."

So, what is the standard of Mahāprabhu's conception? We think 'die to live', that means to give everything. But Mahāprabhu said, kṣaṇeke, that is, 'now, this instant' He is ready to die crores of times if as a result of that He can get Kṛṣṇa. But, Kṛṣṇa is not so cheap. Physical death – that is only to give up the dress, the flesh and bone dress. What is the charm, what is the value, the benefit of that? But to get Kṛṣṇa, it must be something more. It is not that by only some 'negative' sacrifice of what we all possess – the body, by shedding the outer dress – we can go naked to Kṛṣṇa. There must be some positive attraction for Him, and that is the necessary thing. The real thing is to have śraddhā, faith, and sādhu-saṅga, a serving tendency to the devotees. That is to have the 'visa' to go to Him and not just the 'passport'. It is not that by collecting any number of passports I can go, but a visa is necessary, a sanction from that place.

Infinite Resources

The residents of that domain, that divine abode of Kṛṣṇa, are very generous, very loving, and infinitely resourceful. Infinite resources are there, and that is not found in this world. Here, sometimes we see that the government of a particular country tries to oust the immigrants, the 'foreigners'. For so long the government may have been very liberal towards them, but then they find that so many foreigners have come to live there and it is making the indigenous people's life intolerable, so there must be some check on the immigrants. But in the infinite world, there is no such limitation, all may come. The criterion is only, "Come with goodwill. With standard goodwill you should come, and you are all welcome here, infinitely. But you have to give up all your anti-tendencies towards this land – keep them outside, then come. Come for the interest of this land, for the Lord. Come! You are welcome, very earnestly, affectionately, welcome."

Kṛṣṇa is the Lord of all of us, not only a particular section. He is Lord of all, and He is a loving Lord, and He is infinite. His love is infinite, His ways are infinite, everything of Him is infinite. So, in the infinite world there is no thought that "our portion will be less if others come and participate in the service here." Rather, they think, "We want that more and more will be engaged in His service, and we will be more happy. But, be mindful only that you come for service, for His satisfaction – that is the criterion. We are here searching, seeking for His satisfaction, not for the satisfaction of any one of us, and if we find anything lacking in you in that regard, we will turn to become your enemy." With this idea, this understanding, all can come.

The Criterion of Love

So, satisfaction of Kṛṣṇa, of the Centre, is all-in-all in that realm. It is mentioned in *Śrī Chaitanya-charitāmṛta* that Rādhārāṇī says of Her 'opposition-party' leader – though that anti-party is a necessary part of the līlā, the divine play, for the satisfaction of Kṛṣṇa – "She does not know how to satisfy Kṛṣṇa to His heart's content, so why does she venture to come very close to Him? If she could do so, if she could satisfy Him, I would have no objection, rather I would try to bring her to Him, to My Lord. But she fails to do so, to give service to His highest satisfaction. What then? I shall have to go nearer to Him, and for His satisfaction, not for Myself."

Such is the criterion there, though it is inconceivable to us, to our understanding, and it is recorded in *Śrī Chaitanya-charitāmṛta*. Everything is for the satisfaction of Kṛṣṇa. It is all 'Centre-centred' and to the extreme, "If to satisfy Him, the Lord of my heart, I have to serve in a lower way, even like that of a prostitute, I am ready for that." If it is for His satisfaction, although that service may appear as the lowest, it is the highest. There is only one criterion: His satisfaction. Our calculation of what is good or bad has no value there. In this way, among all the servitors, service is drawn up, to the highest position.

ātmendriya-prīti-vāñchhā – tāre bali 'kāma'
kṛṣṇendriya-prīti-ichchhā dhare 'prema' nāma
(Śrī Chaitanya-charitāmṛta: Ādi-līlā, 4.165)

"The desire to gratify one's own senses is kāma (lust), but the desire to please the senses of Lord Kṛṣṇa is prema (love)."

Divine Aspiration

These are all very high things. It is easy to talk of them, but to attain them is very, very difficult. So it is safe for us to realise that one day we may hope to reach so high, though now we are far away. At present, we are in the midst of disappointment. We feel, "I don't like this, I don't feel in a normal position here, I feel dissatisfaction, virakti. I do not know whether my aspiration will be realised, will be fulfilled, any day or other, but still I cannot connect my faith with any other thing, any other conception but the Kṛṣṇa conception. Just because I may be able to get something easily and very quickly, in a day or two, should I make my connection with that? I am not a person to make any such contract. In my quest, in my search, eternal search, I may or I may not get it, but still I won't budge an inch from the ideal that my Lord is Kṛṣṇa in Vṛndāvan, and Kṛṣṇa as the son of mother Yaśodā, the friend of Subāl and others, and the consort of the gopīs and Rādhārāṇī. I want to have the service of that Kṛṣṇa and the service of the servants of His servants – that I adore, I welcome, and not kingship, or leadership, in any sort of mundane achievement."

So, Lord Kṛṣṇa says to Uddhava (*ŚB:* 11.14.14) [1]:

na pārameṣṭhyaṁ na mahendra-dhiṣṇyaṁ
na sārvabhaumaṁ na rasādhipatyam
na yoga-siddhīr apunar-bhavaṁ vā
mayy arpitātmechchhati mad vinānyat

"One who has fixed his consciousness on Me desires neither the position or abode of Lord Brahmā or Lord Indra, nor an empire on thc carth, nor sovereignty in the lower planetary systems, nor the eightfold perfection of yoga, nor liberation from birth and death. Such a person desires Me alone."

Endnotes to Chapter 5

1 Fixing one's consciousness on the Lord and desiring Him alone – this is the goal of all serious spiritual practitioners, something which would appear a mere fantasy to materialists, and one which, since they have made personal or extended (family, society, etc.) sensual/mental/intellectual 'happiness' the supreme goal of life, they would not consider desirable or worthwhile. But whether or not such a spiritual goal is achievable, the transcendental seeker can never abandon it. Here, what is very important is sincerity – one's being clear and straightforward, being honest about oneself. There is no room for duplicity on the spiritual path. All spiritual traditions attest to this. Śrīla Bhakti Siddhānta Saraswatī Ṭhākur, founder of Śrī Gauḍīya Maṭh, was especially strong on this point. Inability or incapacity in following strictly or well the 'spiritual principles', due to personal weakness ("the spirit is willing, but the flesh is weak") is excusable if one is sincere. Hypocrisy, double-dealing, the attempt to cheat others into believing one is a spiritually advanced, saintly, person – that is a matter far more detrimental to one's spiritual life. Ultimately, this is of course only to cheat oneself. The Lord knows everything, and in one way or another this deception will be exposed, and the chance to reform will also be given.

Al-Ghazzali (Abu Hamid Muhammed al-Ghazzali), the renowned Sufi theologian, philosopher, jurist and mystic wrote about the complete surrender to the Lord to which the soul is called, in which there must be an annihilation of the false ego-self in order for the true self to be revealed in all her true glory. This process of 'stripping', Śrīla Śrīdhar Mahārāj referred to as 'die to live', so that one's 'golden self' can emerge. All pretences would be brought to the surface and removed, like impurities when gold alloy is smelted in the crucible. This process Śrīla Rūpa Goswāmī named as anartha-nivṛtti.

In his poem *Only the Lovers will not be Destroyed*, Al-Ghazzali, also known for his common sense, humanism and humour, writes: "On the Day of Judgement, the Lord of Wisdom shall demand of the learned, 'What did you do with the knowledge and learning I gave you?' They will reply, 'We spent it on Your Way.' Then the Lord of Wisdom will say 'You are liars!' And the angels will also say, 'You are liars.' And the Lord of Wisdom will continue, 'You say you spent your knowledge and learning in My Way. Nonsense, you spent it in scavenging for applause, trying to pass yourselves off as savants, and wheedling worship from the masses.' Then the Lord of Magnificence will ask the rich, 'What did you do with the wealth I gave you?' And they will say, 'We gave it away in Your Way.' And the Lord of Magnificence and His angels will say, 'You are lying. You gave it away only so people would call you charitable.' Then the Lord of Power will summon all those who sacrificed their lives in holy wars, and He will ask them, 'How did you spend your life?' And they will reply, 'We gave away our life in Your way.' And the Lord of Power and the angels will laugh and call them liars, and say, 'You sacrificed your life only so people could call you courageous and dub you as martyrs.' Only the lovers, on that Last Day, will not be destroyed."

Note: Al-Ghazzali greatly influenced the mystical poet Rumi, who lived a century or so after him. He is also said to have influenced the development of Christianity in medieval Europe – his were the leading works read by key Christian thinkers, most notably Thomas Aquinas. He was active in Persia during Islam's golden age of progressive enquiry and relatively 'enlightened' rule.

Chapter Six

Restoring Spiritual Health

Hunger of the Spirit

Śrīla Śrīdhar Mahārāj: In the case of the conditioned soul (baddha-jīva), the mind, the intelligence, and the other subtle material tendencies are looting the property of devotion, so devotion is not getting its due. It is starved of its food, its nourishment, and remains always in the minor position. With the help of the revealed scriptures and the saints, we are to improve our condition. 'Where there's a will, there's a way.' We have that tendency for devotion. We have a liking for that life, that property of devotion, it is innate in us, and with their help we can feel it more and more. Ruchi, taste, is the first thing necessary – to have laulyam, hankering, and lobha, greed, for that kind of life. First we must sincerely want it, then the way will be shown to us, and we will get it.[1]

Our hunger must be increased. At present, we are diseased. 'Diseased' means, there is no hunger. We must behave in such a way that our spiritual hunger will be increased, and that is with the help of the healthy persons – the sādhus.

Our spiritual food should be well-adjusted. Proper adjustment with nature, proper food, proper dealings, will help to recover our lost health.[2] On the whole we have to move in such a way, and we will feel within ourselves whether our health is being restored or not. Hṛdayena-abhyanujñāto – our heart will tell us whether our health is improving or is decaying.

Favourable Service

We must be always awake about our internal interest, how to help it, and that interest, that nature, is one of sacrifice, of dedication. Dedication is nobility, it is a noble thing. We must learn to give ourselves for the noble cause. To give, and thereby to thrive. There are also the outer signs of our improvement: anyābhilāṣa-karma-jñāna[3] – no desire for the fruits of service, for enjoyment or for renunciation and liberation. Another great hindrance is slothfulness or idleness, ease-loving. This is an enemy. Instead we should try to live in a plane of energy, of energising. Viṣvanāth Chakravartī Ṭhākur mentions that we should be careful about slackness and a lack of earnestness, they are 'anti-bhakti' and we should not fall prey to them.

Śrīla Rūpa Goswāmī says that in the higher stage of devotion also, we will not like to be connected with the Lord in an 'indirect' way, it is prātikūlya, unfavourable. Our service must be rendered in a favourable way. By any connection with the Lord, we can get out of this conditioned world, but that connection should be favourable, ānukūlyasya saṅkalpa.

Many demons had dealings with the Lord through kāmāt, krodhād, bhayāt, dveṣāt – lust, anger, fear, dread. They were also connected with Kṛṣṇa-līlā, but they were in the opposition party, prātikūlam, and that is never desirable by the śuddha-bhakta, the pure devotee. The devotees don't want to be included amongst the enemies in Kṛṣṇa-līlā, though that is also, in an indirect way, connected with the Lord. Kaṁsa was connected with Him through bhaya-dveṣāt, fear and dread. He was always expecting Kṛṣṇa to kill him, and Siśupāla, through jealousy, wanted to marry Rukmiṇī. Similarly, so many demons like Baka and Pūtanā had relations with the Lord, but that is prātikūlam, unfavourable. Devotees do not like to be aligned with them. Rather, we shall aspire for ānukūlyasya saṅkalpa, a favourable serving-line for Kṛṣṇānuśīlanam, our cultivation of Kṛṣṇa consciousness.

The Positive Side of Reality

Kṛṣṇa consciousness is a dynamic life and not a static conception of the highest life as being 'perfect rest', which is something like 'zero'. The Buddhist conception of nirvāṇa, merging into virajā, and the Śaṅkarite's merging into Brahma, the infinite light, or halo, of the Lord, these are conceptions of that type.[4] But Rāmānuja, Madhva Āchārya, Viṣṇuswāmī, Nimbārka[5], they give the proper interpretation of the positive side of reality, that by a serving attitude we can enter into a new world, and that is the ideal, it is the reality: we thrive by giving, and not by taking, nor by renouncing. In general, that is the desired disposition. So, we shall 'love life'.[6] But what for? Not for the neighbour, not for the country, not the society, but for the Whole. And what is the conception of the Whole? It is not Brahma, nor Paramātmā, not even Nārāyaṇ, but Kṛṣṇa Himself. And what is the difference between these – between Kṛṣṇa, Brahma, Paramātmā, Nārāyaṇ, and so many incarnations of Nārāyaṇ? We have to understand this, and select Kṛṣṇa. And there is differentiation even in the Kṛṣṇa conception: Dwāraka-Kṛṣṇa, Mathurā-Kṛṣṇa, Vṛndāvan-Kṛṣṇa. And, Kṛṣṇa is served by different camps, different sections of devotees – there are so many details. Gradually, through the cultivation of Kṛṣṇa consciousness, Kṛṣṇānuśīlanam, we shall come to understand the differentiated characteristics of Kṛṣṇa.

Endnotes to Chapter 6

1 Śrīla Rūpa Goswāmī writes:

kṛṣṇa-bhakti-rasa-bhāvitā matiḥ
krīyatāṁ yadi kuto 'pi labhyate
tatra laulyam api mūlyam ekalaṁ
janma-koṭi-sukṛtair na labhyate
(Padyāvalī: 14)

"Pure devotional service in Kṛṣṇa consciousness cannot be had even by pious activity in hundreds and thousands of lives. It can be attained only by paying one price – that is, intense greed to obtain it. If it is available somewhere, one must purchase it without delay."

There is an Indian story which illustrates what this 'intense greed' means, and what it demands from the spiritual seeker. Here it is recounted by Anthony de Mello SJ (1931–1987), well known spiritual author and teacher, in one of the last retreat conferences he gave:

"God cannot resist the one who desires Him ardently. I was much impressed by the Hindu story of the villager who came to a sannyāsī (a holy man) while he was meditating under a tree, and said to him, 'I want to see God. Show me how I can experience God.' The sannyāsī, typically, said nothing. He continued with his meditation. The good villager returned with the same request the next day – and the next, and next, and next, though he received no reply until, seeing his perseverance, the sannyāsī at last said to him, 'You seem to be a genuine seeker after God. This afternoon I shall go down to the river for my bath. Meet me there.' When the two of them were in the water, the sannyāsī grasped the head of the man firmly, pushed it under the water and held it there for a couple of minutes while the poor man struggled to come out of the water. After a couple of minutes the sannyāsī released him and said, 'Come again to the banyan tree tomorrow.' When he came the next day it was the sannyāsī who spoke first. 'Tell me,' he said, 'Why did you struggle so much while I held your head under the water?' 'Because,' said the man, 'I was gasping for air – without air I would have died.' Then the sannyāsī smiled and said, 'the day you desire God as desperately as you desired air, you will surely find Him.'"

And de Mello continues: "This is the chief reason why we do not find God: we do not desire Him ardently enough. Our lives are crowded with far too many other things and we can get on pretty well without God. He is certainly not as essential to us as the air we breathe…"

2 "When a man in the material world takes more interest in the materialistic way of life than in Kṛṣṇa consciousness, he is considered to be in the diseased condition. The normal condition is to remain an eternal servant of the Lord (*jīvera svarūpa haya kṛṣṇera nitya-dāsa*). This healthy condition is lost when the living entity forgets Kṛṣṇa due to being attracted by the external features of Kṛṣṇa's māyā energy. This world of māyā is called durāśraya, which means 'false or bad shelter'… Despite this disease, if one with great care and attention takes to Kṛṣṇa consciousness, chanting the Holy Name and hearing Kṛṣṇa's transcendental Pastimes, his ignorance will be destroyed and his tongue enabled to taste the sweetness of the transcendental nature of Kṛṣṇa and His paraphernalia. Such a recovery of spiritual health is possible only by the regular cultivation of Kṛṣṇa consciousness." (Śrīla A.C. Bhaktivedānta Swāmī Prabhupāda, *Upadeśāmṛta*, text 7, purport).

This regular cultivation of Kṛṣṇa consciousness, is essentially effective, however, when carried out in the association of devotees. In the analogy which Śrīla Śrīdhar Mahārāj gives here, the 'spiritually diseased' person has no appetite, no hunger, for spiritual life, Kṛṣṇa consciousness, and he has to recover from this condition by receiving good 'food' from the healthy, the sādhus. But this food must be well-adjusted, that is to say, must be of suitable quality and quantity, according to the nature, and the level of disease, of the unhealthy patient.

As Śrīla Śrīdhar Mahārāj often used the expression, "We must have sympathetic dealings with nature", we must be 'neither miser, nor prodigal' – our life must be balanced, we must follow, as it is termed in the Buddhist language, the 'middle path'. If a person has a capacity to eat and digest only two or three chapatis, if he is given ten chapatis, and even told this will be 'good for him', we can obviously expect that if he consumes them, it will not be conducive to health and may have an adverse reaction in him. So the caring provider, who is sensitive to the person's situation and condition, will feed him accordingly. An infant who is taking breast milk, when he is grown-up a little and is stronger, can be weaned, taken from the breast and given stronger food like grains, in time the child when grown will be able to eat and digest even a large feast.

Good spiritual direction is important, especially at the times of transition in a practitioner's life, because then he is particularly vulnerable. He has been removed from his 'comfort zone' but has not yet fully entered into, or consolidated himself in, his new position. He is, in the phrase first coined by anthropologist Arnold van Geunep, in the 'liminal state' (expressed by Richard Rohr OFM, in his writings, as 'liminal space'). This is a kind of 'no-man's-land' between the habitual use and efficacy of one's own activity, and the infusion of inspiration, through grace, of God. In this space, this 'night of sense' as St. John of the Cross calls it, the consolations and spiritual 'taste' which the soul had received previously, is withdrawn, and nothing the practitioner does in terms of increasing his spiritual practices, brings it back. He may mistakenly think, and feel, that God Himself has withdrawn, abandoned him. He may become convinced that he is going 'backwards', which may cause him great anxiety. But, in fact, God is indeed working in his soul: "The night of sense is a spiritual growing-up process similar to the transition from childhood to adolescence in chronological life. The emotionalism and sentimentality of childhood are beginning to be laid aside in favour of a more mature relationship with God." (Thomas Keating, from his seminal book *Open Mind, Open Heart*, p.26.) This is a testing time of entering and crossing the 'interior desert' in order to reach the 'promised land'. And it occurs not once, but repeats in a cyclic way, at different levels on the 'upward spiral' of the soul's path. In this state, one must simply surrender to the Lord – 'die to live' – in a deeper way, not so much by increasing his spiritual practice quantitatively, but, while maintaining his life of sādhana (practice), to remain at peace and to "abide before God with faith in His presence, continually turning to Him as if opening one's eyes to look at a loved one." (Keating).

3 *Anyābhilāṣa-karma-jñāna*: pure devotional service, means to act favourably and exclusively for the satisfaction of Kṛṣṇa, free from desire for fruits or elevation, and liberation. It is from the verse by Śrīla Rūpa Goswāmī:

anyābhilāṣitā-śūnyaṁ jñāna-karmādy-anāvṛtam
ānukūlyena kṛṣṇānuśīlanaṁ bhaktir uttamā
(Bhakti-rasāmṛta-sindhu: 1.1.11)

"One should render transcendental loving service to the Supreme Lord Kṛṣṇa favourably and without desire for material profit or gain through fruitive activities or philosophical speculation. That is called pure devotional service."

4 Virajā and brahma are taṭasthā; that is, they constitute the 'border land' between the material and spiritual worlds – which is also an infinite plane. Śrīla Śrīdhar Mahārāj sometimes described this as 'abscissa' or 'no-man's-land'. Virajā is the 'moat', a watery substance surrounding the materially differentiated dimension. When the jīva-soul's exploiting tendency is reduced to zero, he (apparently) 'merges' into this region – the Buddhist theory of extinction, or nirvāṇa, i.e. to escape the forest of material entanglement, the world

of repeated birth and death, samsāra. And brahma is the light, the halo or effulgence of the spiritual abode, but again, non-differentiated, being composed of uncountable individual souls, minute sparks of consciousness (anuchetana) but massed together, without differentiation. Sometimes in Vaiṣṇava writings the taṭasthā region is referred to as 'brahma-nirvāṇa'. Though the taṭasthā-śakti is achintya, inconceivable, being beyond the reach of reason or intellect, Śrīla Śrīdhar Mahārāj offered a helpful clarification, that virajā may be conceived of as the 'downwards-facing' aspect of taṭasthā, towards the materially-differentiated world, and brahma as the 'upper-facing' aspect, towards the spiritual, differentiated, world.

5 These are the prominent Āchāryas representing the four Vaiṣṇava sampradāyas, or lineages. Respectively, they are: Rāmānuja, the sampradāya originating from Lakṣmī Devī; Madhva Āchārya, that from Lord Brahmā; Viṣṇu Swāmī, the Rudra-sampradāya from Lord Śiva; and Nimbārka (sometimes called Nimbaditya), that originating from chatuḥsana, the four Kumāra (child) saints, the sons of Lord Brahmā.

6 "So, we shall love life." We shall love life, and we shall not hate it! Devotees will of course try not to live by exploitation of nature or of others, whether 'randomly', or 'piously-organised' (as in the karma-kāṇḍa system of sacrifice). It is impossible for the conditioned-soul to live, to exist at all, without exploiting another, because in the material world, *jīvo-jīvasya-jīvanam*, one living being can only exist at the cost of another. However, we shall not, being acutely aware of this fact, and of the suffering which naturally comes as a reaction to it, out of frustration, 'hate life', and attempt to extinguish our existence in spiritual 'suicide' by merging into brahma-nirvāṇa. Rather, we shall 'love life'.

As Śrīla Śrīdhar Mahārāj often explains, "the environment is your friend", and this will be realised when you are properly adjusted with the Whole, with the Lord. Beginners in spiritual life, when they become acutely aware of the limitations and inebrieties of the conditions of material existence – such as birth, old age, disease and death, to name a few – may initially develop an aversion to the material world, and in their attempts to become detached from it, think they have to 'hate' it. Later they come to a more integrated understanding. Thomas Merton in his writings describes how as a new monk, after long seclusion in his monastery he once had occasion to go into town for a doctor's appointment. He was standing at a busy road crossing watching all the people rushing to and fro in the street like so many ants, and was thinking how empty and pointless their lives were (compared, of course, to his!). Several years later, he happens to be standing at the very same place again but now, with matured understanding, seeing all the people there he felt a great love that he was 'one' with them, that they are all his own beloved family, children of the one loving Lord, God.

So, we shall love life. And that, not for ourself, or for any self-extensions, however broad – family, society, nation, planet, universe – but for the source and the Centre of all things, our loving Lord Kṛṣṇa. (And, very practically, when one is living in the material world – since 'utility is the principle' – one has every opportunity to serve the Lord with 'all the world has to offer'!)

Chapter Seven

Key to the House of Transformation

Hope for the Helpless

In general, what is necessary for us is that our energy may not be utilised against our own development, our own interest. Our energy must not be used against ourself, against the ideal life, the original life, the normal life that we have within us. We must be careful not to be our own enemy. Generally, we are our own enemy because we are living with the 'enemy inside'. Lust, anger, greed, madness, illusion, envy (kāma, krodha, lobha, moha, mada, mātsarya) – we are constantly living with these enemies within. We are surrounded by them always. Whether we are sleeping, moving about, working, or eating, they are within us. Our position is so helpless. We are prey to all these enemies who are living within us, sucking our very blood and going against our own interest. Such a hopeless condition we are in at present.

In this condition, only with the help of our friends can we get relief, so we shall always try to be with our friends. And who are our friends? Those who are trying for a normal life, they are our friends. They are the devotees. And our internal prayer to the Lord, will be fervent, sincere: "Please save me from the hands of these enemies. I am helpless. I have no independence but I am a doll, a play-doll in their hands, this is my hopeless position. How am I to get out of their clutches, my Lord? You are my inner Lord. You are inside me, and they are 'outside'. Please help me from within to get out of their hands."

The wealth, the prospect, is inside us, and when we are free from the clutches of these enemies, we shall be able to see that everything is our friend – we are living in the midst of friends. The whole environment will be changed, transformed, and we will see that it is all-friendly to us.

Course Correction

In a dream, we may see that we are surrounded by enemies, but that is a misconception. We are suffering from misconception. We are surrounded by friends, but because there is something wrong with me, I am only able to see enemies everywhere. That is māyā, misunderstanding, to think "they are all enemy". Their position as 'enemy' is an imaginary position due to wrong thinking within ourselves. When that is corrected, then that wrong conception, that māyic misunderstanding will vanish. That false personification of all as our 'enemy' will go, and they will turn to be our friends. When all misconceived ideas will leave us, even the kāma, krodha, lobha which are tempting us for exploitation, will be our friends. We shall see, "O, they are exciting me for the service of Kṛṣṇa." If there is a kind of food I like very much, that it is very tasteful to my tongue, at that time I will think, "Mahāprabhu likes this very much, so with this food I shall try to serve Him." Or, if a girl is very beautiful, she is attracting me, I shall think, "O, this girl is so beautiful, she will be very valuable in the service of Kṛṣṇa."

In this way self-interest will leave, it will be transformed into God-interest, Kṛṣṇa-interest. It will be for His enjoyment. Everything will be Kṛṣṇa-connected, and through that, satisfaction will come to me: "I have served Kṛṣṇa with this – I am satisfied." That is a different line of satisfaction – satisfaction by supplying different things to the Centre, to Kṛṣṇa.[1]

The Proper Utility of Everything

Nothing is useless, but everything is useful when it is utilised for the proper purpose, for the Centre of all existence, for Kṛṣṇa. That Centre knows what is the proper utility of everything. We are not fit, we have no capacity to know that proper utility, so we have to utilise all our energy for that Centre. We have only to 'supply food to the stomach'. The stomach knows very well how to digest the different types of food, how to prepare them and convert them into nutrients, where to send them, and how much to send – how much to the blood, how much to the brain, how much to the limbs, and so on. So, you are to 'pour water onto the root of the tree' – serve the Centre – and that will be your best service. Try to be practised in that way. All your activities should be adjusted in this line, to pour water onto the root. And don't go into separate negotiations with anyone.[2] If there is any separate negotiation, that is only for advice on how to 'pour water onto the root', how to put food into the stomach. For that sort of advice, we can seek help from outside, from others. But the main principle is, to 'put food in the stomach', and the stomach will make arrangements to distribute that food to all places, as necessary. In this way, our attempt should always be to connect everything with Kṛṣṇa, and through Him, satisfaction and benefit will come to us automatically.[3] This will be the best use of our life-energy.

Energy-Efficient System

Our life is a dependent life. We are always dependent – dependent on Him, on the Lord, and He is the Centre, the Centre of all existence. 'Centre' means, not alone – it is a system, a government. It works through different positions, different camps, or agents. You will submit to the Centre through them, and through them, also, energy will come to you. On the whole, your consciousness will be that you shall give your whole energy to the Centre through those who are real agents of the Centre, who are really connected with Him. From your present position you shall try as much as you can to practise this, to utilise your energy in this way. Your energy must go to the Centre, but according to your present position – that is, not directly but through a particular system, and that is through guru to Kṛṣṇa. You are not sufficiently powerful to connect with the Absolute Centre directly, at once, at any moment, in any way, so you must learn how to aspire after this approach to Him. Then, the result will come to you as necessary for you in your present position, again through the agency, through guru. But, your connection is with the Centre.

Stages of Progress

In this way our approach must be systematic, not haphazard. First, you must learn what to want. What is your prospect in life, for what should you seek? In the stage of śravaṇa-daśā, by giving careful attention, hearing about Kṛṣṇa consciousness and its different prospects, we begin our search.

Then, varaṇa-daśā, the selection: "These are the different prospects extended to me, what should I select?" There are different rasas: śānta, dāsya, sakhya, vātsalya, mādhurya. After hearing about all such prospects, now in the varaṇa-daśā stage we have to make our selection, and to accept the agent for that, with the internal approval of our heart. Hṛdayena-abhyanujñāto: "Yes, this is it, this is where I belong, my own real self. For whom I was searching for so long, I have found it here! Here, I have found my guide. I can rely on him. I can place myself at his disposal, then my fortune will be increased, and guaranteed."

Then sādhana-daśā: the proper practices, and the progress, will begin in our life.

Gradually we shall feel our 'home environment': "Yes, I am coming home, I am feeling this to be my home." This is the stage of prāpana-daśā – to feel our home.

Next there is āpana-daśā, that is, to help others also come to their home.

These are the stages of progress, and they are all included in sambandha-jñāna, that is, the estimation of our self and of the environment: "Who am I? Where am I, what is my position at present, and what should be my ultimate destination? And how to attain that?"

Our practical engagement towards that goal is abhidheya or the 'means to the end'. Then, prayojana, the goal.

In that goal, that destination, what will be our renumeration, our 'salary' there? Śrī Chaitanya Mahāprabhu prays, "*Dāsa' kari' vetana more deha prema-dhana.*[5] My salary will be loving service" – we will have more love, more affection, to march forward, more energy to march towards that destination. Our vetana, salary, our inner salary will be increased energy to discharge our duty.

So, sambandha-jñāna is the foundation. It is analysis of the environment and our own position. That 'environment' includes many things including the relationships of the master, the friend, and the servant. With this understanding we are to march on, abhidheya. Then prayojana, the goal, the attainment, the payment.

Under these three headings, sambandha, abhidheya, prayojana we have to understand things, in a systematic way.

Endnotes to Chapter 7

[1] It is the nature of the spirit-soul, jivātmā, to be always seeking enjoyment (*ānanda-mayo 'bhyāsāt*). The conditioned soul seeks such 'directly', that is, through the contact of his material senses with their objects (eye for form, ear for sound, skin for touch, etc.) but the satisfaction gained thereby is not only of a temporary nature, but also reactionary.

However, by "supplying different things to Krsna", the soul is having a "different line of enjoyment". He is enjoying, but through satisfying Krsna his own joy and satisfaction are there, and it is of a much deeper and more lasting nature. *Hṛṣīkena Hṛṣīkeśa-sevanaṁ bhaktir uchyate* (*Bhakti-rasāmṛta-sindhu*: 1.1.12). It is in fact, the natural position of the soul to be the 'second' or 'secondary' enjoyer – he enjoys, or better to say, relishes what has been first enjoyed by Krsna, the Supreme Enjoyer. (Because of its common usage, it is difficult to separate the word 'enjoyment' from some meaning or sense of 'exploitation'; Śrīla Śrīdhar Mahārāj generally did not like to even use the word when referring to 'spiritual satisfaction'.) What to speak of the remnants of the Lord, pure devotees, as voiced by Śrī Uddhava to Lord Kṛṣṇa, in *Śrīmad Bhāgavatam*, 11th Canto, always like to live on the remnants – food, garlands, clothes, articles – of the Vaiṣṇavas, the Lord's devotees.

2 "Separate negotiations with anyone." One will not seek spiritual advice from others, those outside the line of devotional service, as understood from the teachings of Vaiṣṇava śāstras such as *Bhagavad-gītā*, *Śrīmad Bhāgavatam*, and the teachings of Śrī Chaitanya Mahāprabhu. The philosophical/theological ideas and speculations of others can deviate an inexperienced devotee from the devotional path. (If the conclusions of others, for example those practising within other genuine theistic faith-traditions, are 'in the line of' exclusive devotion to, and service of, the Supreme Lord, according to their own understanding of Him, that of course can be appreciated. The good examples of such persons, can even inspire and encourage the devotee in his own path. But here also, one must have proper discrimination and maturity, to avoid confusion.
In such a situation, one unsure is better advised to seek advice from respected seniors.)

3 We are reminded of the words of the Gospel where Christ says: "But seek Ye first the Kingdom of God, and His righteousness, and all these things shall be added unto you." *(Matt. 6:33, King James Bible)*

Note: This appears in the *Sermon on the Mount* chapters 5 to 7 of St. Matthew's gospel, and really it contains the essence of Christ's message. In it, are included the famous 'Beatitudes' ("Blessed are the poor in spirit, for theirs is the Kingdom of Heaven", etc.); and Jesus goes on to explain the illimitable goodness of the Father-God, and illuminate through many examples, how one should have complete trust and confidence in Him. While not expressed in terms which meet the depth and sophistication of Vaiṣṇava theology, these verses stand out for their beauty and simplicity. From the lips of Jesus Christ, certainly an empowered representative of the Lord, they have the ability to penetrate the heart and change lives. As the

Sermon ends: "And it came to pass, when Jesus had ended these sayings, the people were astonished at his doctrine: for he taught them as one having authority, and not as the scribes."
(*Matt.* 7, 28–29)

4 The Sanskrit word 'rasa' cannot be very easily or satisfactorily translated into the English language. As expressed by Śrīla A.C. Bhaktivedānta Swāmī Prabhupāda, 'rasa' means 'mellow', or 'taste' – as in, the 'taste of loving devotion' (Bhakti-rasa). Since 'rasa' or 'taste' is intrinsic to relationship, the five primary and seven secondary spiritual relationships which the soul may have with the Lord are described as 'rasas'. In a discussion between Śrīla Bhakti Siddhānta Saraswatī Ṭhākur, founder of Śrī Gauḍīya Maṭh, and Professor Dr. P. Johanns, religious instructor in Jesuit Studies at St. Xaviers College, Calcutta, which took place in April of 1928, in answer to the Professor's enquiry "Could you define 'rasa'?" Śrīla Saraswatī Ṭhākur replied: "Śrī Rūpa Goswāmī gives us a definition for 'rasa' in his *Bhakti-rasāmṛta-sindhu*. The rasa we are discussing is not mundane rasa. Mundane rasa is the perverted, abominable, and incomplete reflection of spiritual, transcendental rasa. His definition of rasa is as follows (as quoted in *Śrī Chaitanya-charitāmṛta: Ādi-līlā, 10.58*):

vyatītya bhāvanā-vartma
yaś chamatkāra-bhāra-bhūḥ
hṛdi sattvojjvale bāḍhaṁ
svadate sa raso mataḥ

"That which is beyond imagination, heavy with wonder, and relished in a heart shining with goodness is known as rasa."

Śrīla Saraswatī Ṭhākur went on to elaborately describe something of the operation of the rasas in relation to both the aiśvarya (opulence) and mādhurya (sweet) aspects or manifestations of the Lord, and he ended: "The perverted reflection of this supremely relishable original reality is the temporary, abominable, mundane rasa. We cannot attribute any abomination to Śrī Kṛṣṇa. Śrī Kṛṣṇa's

Pastimes with the gopīs of Vṛndāvan are not a product of this material kingdom. We cannot realise His Pastimes as long as our intelligence is absorbed in even a tinge of matter."

(Dr. Johanns had studied the Vaiṣṇava teachings, specially the works of Śrīla Jīva Goswāmī, was a regular reader of *The Harmonist* journal edited by Śrīla Saraswatī Ṭhākur and had even learnt Sanskrit to advance his studies in Indian philosophy. He respectfully asked many other questions to Śrīla Saraswatī Ṭhākur and was very satisfied with his answers. Śrīla Saraswatī Ṭhākur gifted the Professor with several important Vaiṣṇava books for his library.)

5 **prema-dhana vinā vyartha daridra jīvana**
'dāsa' kari' vetana more deha prema-dhana

(Śrī Chaitanya-charitāmṛta, Antya-līlā: 20.37)

"Without love of Godhead, My life is useless. Therefore I pray that You accept Me as Your servant and give Me the salary of ecstatic love of God."

Part II

The Journey Home

from informal discourses
by
Śrīla Bhakti Rakṣak Śrīdhar
Dev-Goswāmī Mahārāj

With contemporary endnote explanations by
Śrī Bhakti Swarūp Tridaṇḍi Mahārāj

Chapter Eight

Affectionate Connection

Break the Spell

Mostly we are captured by the allurement of the external appearance of things, of the 'cover', of that which we can grasp with our senses – the eye, ear, tongue, the touch, the nose – we are captivated there, and that is the danger. But we must pierce though the coverings to find out and come in connection with what is within, with the truth proper. All our apparent charm for the coverings must be broken to pieces and removed. We are to dive deep into the innermost substance within us, and get back our real connection with Him, with our Lord. Ignoring the coverings over our own selves, the outer representations of body and mind, we must look to the necessity of our deeper person, our real self within. At the same time, piercing through all the coverings of the environment, that which we see outside ourselves, in the world, we shall also try to connect with the innermost substance. These coverings must both be eliminated. That is to say, not 'eliminated' altogether, but we must go through them, to discover the substance within, and that substance's own real interest, then we shall be able to have proper knowledge and proper adjustment, both inner and outer – proper adjustment with the whole.[1]

In short, making too much of the outer representation of things, and ignoring the inner substance, is bad. We are ignoring the soul, the conscious entity, the knower. In the material aspect of our existence also, both gross and subtle, our understanding is also maladjusted – we are making much of the physical body, but ignoring the mind, and ignoring the intelligence, the valuable faculty of judgment within us.

The Wealth Within

If we are too much busy with the external covering of ourselves – the body, flesh and bone – we will be misguided. And in relation to the environment, if we concentrate only on the 'outside', on the external appearance of things, that is to ignore the truth, because within, there is so much of value, there is immense wealth to be had. A man with a good body but not a good mental system, what is his position? His body is good-looking, but there is derangement of his mentality, no good judgment faculty, no magnanimity of heart – he is lacking in all such good qualities. That is a very deficient condition, because the wealth is within. Similarly in our experience of the world, we are to know that the real wealth is within, and we must not allow ourselves to be charmed by the cover, by whatever appears to us on the outside. In this way we are to move in our vision, in our understanding, from deep, to deeper, to deepest, and we must be benefited.

The Five Dimensions of Knowledge

In the scriptures, knowledge has been classified into five planes or stages: pratyakṣa, parokṣa, aparokṣa, adhokṣaja, and aprākṛta.

Pratyakṣa means our sense-experience, that which we gather from the direct experience of our senses. That is our own experience, knowledge which is confined within the limits of our sense-experience.

But if we want to develop further, to grow in our knowledge, then we have to also accept the experience of others. This is called parokṣa, the second plane of knowledge. For example, in medical science there is the discovery or 'invention' of different medicines, and we may get the benefit of such developments. This is not the result of our direct experience, but is the experience of an expert, and we can have the utility and the benefit of that.[2]

'Like a Deep and Peaceful Sleep'

The third type of knowledge, which is of a still higher plane, is called aparokṣa. This may be conceived to be something like the experience of a sound sleep. When we are in a deep, dreamless slumber, we can come in touch with a plane which is not within the experience either of myself, or of others. When in deep sleep, we have no consciousness of that state, but when we come back, when we awaken from it, we sometimes assert, "O, I had a very good sleep, a very happy, peaceful sleep."

There is some sort of inexplicable experience of happiness there, in that plane, some experience of peace is to be traced there. Though it is indistinct, it is hazy, still it is beyond the jurisdiction both of my own direct sense experience, and of the experience of others, be they so many 'experts' of the world. So, aparokṣa is that kind of experience where the subject and material object come together, and the object appears to 'merge' into, to vanish into, the subject. It is the third plane of knowledge. Śankara Āchārya, the great proponent of impersonalism, explains the gradations of consciousness up to this point.

The Transcendental Plane

Above this is turīya, the fourth plane of knowledge, known as adhokṣaja, the transcendental plane. It has been revealed through the great devotee-scholar Śrī Rāmānuja Āchārya, as well as other Vaiṣṇava Āchāryas. It is adhokṣaja, that is, existing beyond the scope of the senses, whether gross or subtle. It is a plane that we can experience only when, by its sweet will, it comes down to our gross stage of understanding – and if it withdraws, we are helpless, we can't find it.

As the soul, we are the thinker, the feeler, and as a subject we conceive of other 'things' of the world as objects of our knowledge. But there is a higher Subject than us, and that 'Super-Subject' is the seer, the feeler, and the knower of myself, but I cannot know Him because the plane of His existence is so fine, my knowing capacity cannot rise up and penetrate into it. My knowing-principle is gross, and that plane is so subtle, so fine – it can come down to contact with me, but I cannot go up, to contact with Him. In this way, I may be handled by Him, by that transcendental Substance and Existence, the super-subjective Existence, the Supersoul. When that plane comes down to contact me, I may have some experience of it, and when it is withdrawn, I can only carry the memory of that, nothing else. I cannot give any 'proof' of its existence, by any will or acumen of my own, I am helpless to do that – because it has withdrawn. I cannot stand in the 'witness-box' and give evidence for it, to prove my case, because the fact that I am referring to is no longer there, it has gone! But, at the same time, we cannot deny its existence.

There is such a possibility that we can experience that higher Existence, and those of us who have such experience, cannot deny it. And that Existence is fully independent – when by its sweet will it withdraws, we cannot force it to remain under our command.

All Powerful and Independent

So, adhokṣaja is the fourth plane of knowledge, the fourth dimension of consciousness. It is beyond our experience. We are, as it were, 'underground', and real knowledge is above, on the surface. That plane is beyond our experience, but if the thick coverings walling up our consciousness, our experience, can be pierced through, then we can come in connection with it.

Adho-kṛtam indriya-jam jñānam: adhokṣaja means the superior knowledge which can overcome, can suppress or 'force down' our knowledge of the experience of this world. It is transcendental, supra-mental knowledge. That plane is not similar to this world, it is different in every way. It is grand, all-powerful, and all-inspiring. It is known as Vaikuṇṭha, the unlimited spiritual region of awe and power.

Pure Love's Domain

Through *Śrīmad Bhāgavatam* and Śrī Chaitanya Mahāprabhu we come to know there is yet a fifth stage, a fifth dimension of knowledge and it has a peculiar characteristic: it is very similar to this mundane world, yet it is not mundane. It is called aprākṛta. It is the most fully-fledged theistic conception, which is only found in Kṛṣṇa's domain, Goloka.

Central knowledge of the Absolute must have a connection with all, even the lowest level of the mundane creation and existence. It must be able to harmonise the worst portion of the illusory world. That knowledge, that plane, is called aprākṛta, supra-mundane.

To enter that highest realm is possible only through divine love. Everything can be compensated for through love. There is a saying that, 'a loving mother thinks her blind child has beautiful lotus eyes'. She is 'blinded' by affection. So, what is mean and low, can be compensated for by love, and like a precious ornament, this shines very beautifully – and that is prema, divine love. Through mercy, through pity, through grace, a King can come to play with a boy on the street. Affection can make it possible, and the difference between high and low disappears at such a stage.

Vṛndāvan Life

The purest devotion is *jñāna-sūnya-bhakti*, divine love which is free from any calculation and does not consider even the opulence and power of the Lord. This is above Vaikuṇṭha, and it goes on under the spell of Yogamāyā, the spiritually-enchanting potency. It is the special art of Yogamāyā that those holding the highest position, think themselves very insignificant. So the residents of Kṛṣṇa's abode, Vṛndāvan, do not know, they are not conscious of their own exalted position, they think themselves ordinary. Love removes the difference of great and small, high and low, and their love is free from any trace of calculation. Vṛndāvan is such a plane of existence.

This is the beautiful nature of the aprākṛta realm, of Vṛndāvan life: it is great without the attitude, the air, of bigness.

Although the residents are really great, they appear to be simple. Power dressed in affection and love, and couched in humility – such is Vṛndāvan, and it is above Vaikuṇṭha, the plane of awe, reverence, power, and opulence.

Śrīmad Bhāgavatam and Śrī Chaitanya Mahāprabhu say this is the highest and most laudable place for us to live. There, the Supreme Lord Kṛṣṇa and the gopīs are living in the forest. We find no grandeur or big buildings there, but if we have a true eye for grandeur, we will see it in Vṛndāvan. From an impartial judgement of the facts, their position is very great, but through humility they have apparently descended to our level. It is a very sweet and beautiful form of life that we find in Vṛndāvan. And Mahāprabhu came to show us that, through *Śrīmad Bhāgavatam*. Kṛṣṇa is the Lord of that land, and the cows, hills, forests and the Yamunā river are all creating a favourable environment there.

Relief from Mania: "Go Home!"

Śrī Chaitanya Mahāprabhu took sannyās[3] to teach us and to take us up and make us the permanent inhabitants of that place. He says that actually our real self lives in that plane, but unfortunately our consciousness has become focused outside. Now we are captured by the mundane aspect of this creation and think that we are suffering, but this is all illusion. We must get relief from this mania. Just as a madman leaves his home and wanders in the street collecting pieces of paper and cloth, so we are focused in this world, but when this madness is gone, we will awaken in our own home.

Mahāprabhu tells us, "You must return home, back to Godhead. You must go home. Your home is such a beautiful land, you must only try for that. At the bottom of all your troubles is the fact that you have identified yourself with this material world and this body of flesh and blood. You have to retrace your path and go back to your home. That is what is necessary."

Śrī Chaitanya Mahāprabhu's sannyās is for all of us. It is for the purpose of taking us back home, where we can have home comforts, home sweetness. If we have any 'home-consciousness' within us, we cannot but appreciate such a proposal. Home, sweet home!

Endnotes to Chapter 8

1 "Proper adjustment with the whole" – that is, with the Whole, the Lord, meaning a proper relationship (sambandha jñāna) with the Lord and His energies.

2 This parokṣa-jñāna, knowledge gleaned from others' experience, may in a more general sense refer not only to expert or specialised knowledge such as that of medical science, etc. but also to whatever may be valuably learned from others. For example, I may have never in my present life been to China, but I can understand something about China, its climate, customs, food, geography and so on by hearing from a friend – who, of course, I trust – who has actually been there. This way my knowledge can expand. (Caveat: in the modern day, unfortunately, many things may be heard or learned from others, that are not necessarily factual at all, but may be given out as false propaganda, and so on. Due to this aberration – the propensity to cheat others is one of the faults of the condition soul, along with imperfect senses, committing mistakes, and being in illusion – this Age of Kali, as well as being the Age of 'quarrel and hypocrisy', was also often described by Śrīla Śrīdhar Mahārāj as the Age of 'doubt and suspicion'.)

[3] Lord Śrī Chaitanya Mahāprabhu is the direct incarnation of the Supreme Lord, Kṛṣṇa, who appears in every kali-yuga as the Yuga-Avatār, the Incarnation of the Age, to teach the chanting of the Holy Name of Kṛṣṇa (the yuga-dharma of the age, or religion of this age). In this particular kali-yuga (coming just once in each day of Lord Brahmā), Mahāprabhu is actually the combined form of Kṛṣṇa and Rādhā, the Complete Absolute. That is, He is Kṛṣṇa Who has assumed the golden colour and inner mood of love of Śrī Rādhā, His internal pleasure-potency (*hlādinī-śakti*), in order to experience and understand the depth of devotion and bliss which She experiences in loving Him.

In His Pastimes on earth (1486–1535 AD), Lord Chaitanya lived as a gṛhasta, a married householder, in Nabadwīp, West Bengal, and in his 24th year took sannyās, the renounced order of life, in order to deliver Love of God to all. He spent six years preaching all over India, and the last 12 years of His manifest presence in near seclusion in Jagannath Purī, Orissa. For an in-depth look at Lord Chaitanya's sannyās, its reasons and inculcation, we would recommend Śrīla Śrīdhar Mahārāj's profound illuminations in his book about the life of Lord Chaitanya: *The Golden Volcano of Divine Love*, pp.95–135.

Chapter Nine

The Highest Solution

Our Eternal Good

So much energy is given for the national cause – so many atomic bombs, so many soldiers ready to devote their life, to sacrifice their life, for the national interest. But this national prosperity, how little it is! What does it amount to? It is trifling. It is as nothing.

The eternal good, however, is real wealth, fortune. It is a good for eternity. So, how much energy should we collect for that? To do good for all, to distribute such fortune, such eternal good to one and all so that they may get back to their Home, to take all the misguided people back to their sweet, sweet, Home – it is such a high degree of welfare. And that is the duty, the call that arose in the mind of Mahāprabhu: "All these vagabonds, they should be taken to their own Home and Guardian. They are wandering here, like so many beasts in the jungle, without knowing what is good or what is bad, and always engaged in some sort of competition, biting one another. Such is their condition, their deplorable condition. I must take them Home."

This is the situation of the souls wandering in this world. And they think they are civilised! Animals who live in the jungle are fighting and biting, all trying to livc, to survivc at thc cost of the others – and human beings, they are following the same course, and more efficiently, fighting other nations. What sort of civilisation is this? It is only a 'civilised jungle'. Then 'civilisation' loses its meaning. 'Civil' means gentle. Is this gentleness?

What one does individually – competition, exploitation, all ungentle behaviour – if one does it as a group, as a nation, does that make it civilisation? And they are proud of doing that kind of activity, and so foolish that they think that by doing it in the name of 'the nation' all such actions are purified, that if their 'jungle habits' can be performed under this name, they are justified. But all these justifications, they are just 'words in a fool's dictionary'.

Help from Home

It is said that a 'half-truth is worse than a lie'. Similarly, a 'half-help', misguided help, that is more dangerous, because it directs one's attention to the wrong thing. Mahāprabhu said,

> **veda nā māniyā bauddha haya ta' nāstika**
> **vedāśraya nāstikya-vāda bauddhake adhika**
> *(Śrī Chaitanya-charitāmṛta, Madhya-līlā: 6.168)*

"The Buddhists do not recognise the authority of the Vedas, therefore they are considered agnostics. However, those who have taken shelter of the Vedic scriptures yet preach agnosticism in accordance with the māyāvāda philosophy are certainly more dangerous than the Buddhists."

In the name of religion, if we preach atheism, that is more dangerous than the preaching of a 'street-atheist'.[1] In the name of 'civilisation', societies and nations are doing what is shameful even for the animals of the jungle. They are giving food and clothing, and so-called education, to the public, and that is supposed to be a very good thing, a high thing. But that is not even a 'half-truth'. But to take them Home, and nothing less, that is what is necessary.

There is an expression, 'home-comfort'. It means, where it is very sweet. 'Home' means where there is mother, there is father, and they know the real necessity of the child. The child may not know that, but those in his home know what is his real interest. His mother, father, and so many affectionate relatives, they know more than the boy himself. So, the real necessity is to guide the person to their Home, and there the whole atmosphere will automatically come to help them, to render real help to them. 'Home' means this, and so we must all go back to God, back to Home.

That was Mahāprabhu's wish. And the duty undertaken by Him: "All the wanderers in the street should be collected and taken Home."

Devotee: Sometimes when preaching to the public, we find it very difficult because they don't want to 'go back Home'! So how should a devotee keep up his enthusiasm for this attempt?

Śrīla Śrīdhar Mahārāj: It depends to some extent on the capacity of the preacher, the guide, the teacher. But somehow, by any means, by 'hook or by crook', we must try to take them Home. There, the Lord knows their best interest, He will see for their 'home comfort'. That is the idea. The child does not know his own real interest, he may be crazy, he may run this way and that, any way but towards home – and this is the problem. It makes the situation very complex, otherwise to take him home would have been very simple! But somehow we must try to take them towards their Home.

Prime Necessity

Whatever is done with the sincere wish of spreading the teachings of Mahāprabhu, that is welcome, and that is Mahāprabhu's instruction: *yāre dekha, tāre kaha 'Kṛṣṇa'-upadeśa*[2] – wherever we go and whomever we find, we shall talk to them about Kṛṣṇa. Kṛṣṇa is the universal Lover and Owner, the Absolute Lord of everyone. So, any time and place, wherever and whenever – whether we are lying down, or taking food, or talking – always, we shall try to connect them with Kṛṣṇa.[3]

That is Mahāprabhu's instruction: "From this mortal world, try to connect them to the highest immortal plane, and not only of immortal existence, but of immortal nectar. Try to connect every mortal being with the Centre of all existence – with Kṛṣṇa. Every atom, every soul, every point of existence, that you come across, connect them with that highest Centre of Love."

This should be done by a sincere devotee. He will try his best to connect Kṛṣṇa with everything. His whole time may be utilised in the connection of Kṛṣṇa, the universal Lord of Love, and he will try to distribute Him to every heart who is suffering from mortality here.

That is Mahāprabhu's desire: "Save them! Save them by spreading the talk of their loving Lord. Kṛṣṇa is the Lord of highest love, the Lord of every soul, and to connect them with Him will be the solution, the highest solution for every life."

Sincere in Service

So, as much as is done for Him, to spread His connection, His association, that is to be appreciated. Every atom must be given that chance. But, we must be sincere. In a diplomatic way, in that attempt, we must not seek our own material aspiration, material gain. That should be eliminated, and there must be only the pure thing: service for sādhu, for guru, and for Kṛṣṇa. With this spirit, whatever is done, it will be useful, and useful not only to me, and not only to the association[4] but to the whole world – to bring the Infinite Good into the finite world, and to connect souls under mortality with Him, as much as we are able to do.

Just as in a famine, as much food as we can distribute to the needy, it is so much the better, so here in this world, where the dearth of Kṛṣṇa consciousness, the lack of real love of the Lord, is very great, we shall try to distribute it to whomever we meet, to one and all.

Nectar-Connection

So, we shall distribute the nectar of Kṛṣṇa consciousness to everyone. We shall try to give them that connection. By doing this, not only the human beings but so many trees, animals, insects, they also may be engaged, and benefitted. The milk we get, we offer to the Lord, and the cows are benefitted. The flowers we take, they go to the Lord, and the tree is benefitted. In any way, whatever we use, water or anything, we offer to the Lord, then sukṛti comes to them and gives some connection towards Kṛṣṇa, and one day they will come to be with Him.

So, try to be the agent, try to work as the agent of Kṛṣṇa consciousness, Kṛṣṇa-affection, and that may be also up to Kṛṣṇa-love of the higher order, as that of the gopīs[5]. That degree, that quality of love which the gopīs have is of very rare value, and that connection should be given to one and all – we shall be agents, wholesale agents for that. And wc shall get renumeration for that 'agent's work' in terms of Kṛṣṇa consciousness, love of Kṛṣṇa – we shall be paid in that coin for our labour in distributing it to others.

A Holy Exchange

Devotee: Śrīla Guru Mahārāj, when we give people prasādam, it seems it is easier for them to accept that, than when we try to collect donations from them. But does this mean that they earn more 'sukṛti'[6] by giving the donation?

Śrīla Śrīdhar Mahārāj: In the case of the general people, when they are given prasādam, there is the chance of them making offence, they may commit aparādha, because they may not take it in the proper mood. If there is not respect, proper regard, there may be offence against prasādam, that is sevā-aparādha (offence in service).

But in the case of taking donations, what you have collected from someone and taken to a proper Vaiṣṇava who will be able to utilise it in service, to give the proper connection with Kṛṣṇa, that is sure. The benefit is sure because the donor's energy, knowingly or unknowingly, is coming into Kṛṣṇa's connection. But with prasādam, a person may not take it in a proper mood. He may feel hate, or he may mix it with other things and then take it – in this way there may be a chance of 'mal-service', aparādha. Prasāda-sevā, that is a kind of service. To take prasādam means to honour it, not to consume it.

Everything that is connected with Kṛṣṇa should be approached in a mood of service. Sukṛti derives from this, and

then this develops into śraddhā, faith. So, according to the degree of a soul's śraddhā, they will take prasādam very earnestly and very reverently, lovingly, and according to that, the consequence, the result, will come to them. Do you follow?
Devotee: Yes.
Śrīla Śrīdhar Mahārāj: So with prasādam, there may be sevā-aparādha, it is possible. But there is no possibility of aparādha in the 'primary' case when a person initially is to earn some sukṛti through contact with a devotee, such as when a devotee collects something from him. The person is giving something and he does not know, he does not understand, for what purpose that is going to be used by the agent, the devotee, for the service of Kṛṣṇa – but he is being benefitted. In this case there is no possibility of aparādha, and even the smallest contribution a person makes is to his or her benefit.

With Due Care

Sometimes, if it is a large contribution, that also may be risky. It may be heavy for the donor. He may not give it with śraddhā, with faith, so that may not fetch such sukṛti leading to devotion.[7] So, the smaller collection, smaller donation, that is safe. The giver does not mind giving a small amount, so there is less possibility of hatred or contempt in their giving, and the result is sukṛti, to their benefit. That is safe for the primary section, the complete newcomers.[8]

But in general, whether it is the case of a book given, or the Śālagrāma-śilā, or Giridhārī, or the Archa-mūrti, or the mālā,[9] if these are treated hatefully, or mishandled, there is the possibility of bad reaction. So the result will come as good or bad – the manner of their use will fetch good or bad for the person receiving them. If they acquire some apathy about any such article, if they hatefully neglect them, that is 'aparādha', and has its bad result.[10]

Delegated Potency

In any case, all the souls wandering under 'māyā' must be taken Home. This is the responsibility of the guide, and according to the guide's capacity, the real result will come, and have its effect. Their special capacity, also their inspiration, which is the special delegation of the Lord – both of these combined, creates the specific characteristic in an Āchārya.

"Rank is but the guinea-stamp, man is the gold for that." There may be so many administrators, district magistrates, judges, and so on, but rank is one thing, and the man is another. The inner capacity, as well as the delegation, empowerment, both of these combined is what is effective. The personal characteristic of the preacher, and the delegation, the delegated power of the Lord, how much power is delegated to him, the combination of these produces the desired result.[11]

Devotee: We know that Kṛṣṇa is coming through the Āchārya…

Śrīla Śrīdhar Mahārāj: That means, His power. 'Kṛṣṇa' here means His delegated power, His potency. Kṛṣṇa is extending His potency, and Kṛṣṇa and Kṛṣṇa's potency are almost one and the same.

Endnotes to Chapter 9

1 If, under the guise of 'true religion' – meaning, an authentic theistic conception, which is based on faith in the eternal, infinite

God the Person, as He is revealed through a genuine tradition – if what is being preached is actually agnosticism, or atheism, in the form of the conclusions of 'nirviśeṣa' and 'sūnyavāda', impersonalism or voidism, especially when this is propagated systematically under the supposed authority of a 'spiritual organisation' or mission, then this is worse, more misleading, than the preaching of an independent 'street atheist' whose views can be more easily dismissed ("it is just his 'opinion'"). This phenomenon is in the present day found among groups claiming to represent lineages of 'yoga' and 'Vedānta', etc.

2 **yāre dekha, tāre kaha 'kṛṣṇa'-upadeśa**
āmāra ājñāya guru hañā tāra' ei deśa
(Śrī Chaitanya-Charitāmṛta: Madhya-līlā, 7.128)

"Whomever you see, wherever you go, tell them about Kṛṣṇa. In this way become a spiritual master and try to liberate everyone in this land."

Śrīla Śrīdhar Mahārāj expresses this verse: "Whomever you find, talk with him only about Kṛṣṇa. We have no other engagement. Whomever you find, any soul you come across, try to save him from this desert of mortality. I command you! Don't be afraid. Take the position of guru, the giver, and give it to everyone."

3 Śrīla Śrīdhar Mahārāj is here saying that whatever the devotee of Mahāprabhu is doing – eating, resting, etc. – he, as the giver, the preacher, should try to connect others with Kṛṣṇa and Kṛṣṇa consciousness. There is a verse in *Śrī Chaitanya Bhāgavat* by Śrīla Vṛndāvan Dās Ṭhākur:

ki śayane, ki bhojane, ki vā jāgaraṇe
aharniśa chinta kṛṣṇa, balaha vadane
(Śrī Chaitanya Bhāgavat: Madhya-khaṇḍa, 28.28)

"Whether you are sleeping, eating, or awake, day and night always think of Kṛṣṇa and chant Kṛṣṇa's Name."

[4] i.e. those in the immediate association of the preacher – the person or persons he or she is preaching to.

[5] The cow-herd maidens of Vraja (Vṛndāvan).

[6] *Sukṛti*: spiritual benefit derived from the blessing of Kṛṣṇa as facilitated through His agent, the Vaiṣṇava. Sukṛti in its matured stage becomes śraddhā, or faith.

[7] In the case of a larger donation, the person requested may feel pressured, or they may donate not wanting to disappoint the devotee but inwardly feeling some resentment. They may offer it grudgingly or with disrespect. Because it is not being offered, to use the English expression, 'in good faith' – faith in this general sense, rather than specifically śraddhā – then it will not accrue any sukṛti, spiritual merit, for them. The mood in which the donation is offered, is important. (In the Bible, there is the statement, "The Lord loves a cheerful giver.")

[8] Traditionally in India, the student monk (brahmachārī) would go on collection for the spiritual master. This was known as 'mādhukarī' – that is, like the bee ('madhu', honey) which takes a little from each flower before going on to the next, thus not accepting too much from any one person, possibly inviting some negative reaction.

[9] *Sālagrām-śilā*: The Deity-stone form of Lord Viṣṇu, derived from the Kali Gaṇḍakī River in Nepal, and traditionally worshipped in India by brāhmaṇas according to strict principles.

Giridhārī: Kṛṣṇa is famous as 'Giridhārī', the lifter of Govardhan Hill (see *Śrīmad Bhāgavatam,* 10:10). Govardhan Hill, in Vṛndāvan, is itself considered to be a form of Kṛṣṇa, and the Govardhan-śilā (stone) from Govardhan Hill is a worshipable Deity Form of the Lord.

Archā-mūrti: the Deity Form of Lord Viṣṇu or Lord Kṛṣṇa.

Mālā: The rosary of 108 beads used by Vaiṣṇavas in private chanting of the Holy Name of Kṛṣṇa.

10 The 'bad result' for the disrespectful receiver. However, the scriptures exhort that the preacher (generally the madhyama-adhikārī, middle level devotee) should not preach to faithless persons for this may invite a negative reaction in such people, and that will be hindrance for the devotee's own spiritual progress. (This is the 'ninth offence against the Holy Name' mentioned in the *Padma Purāṇa*.) The proper recipients of a devotee's preaching are those who are enquiring genuinely and sincerely, or who are curious, or inoffensive. The envious or atheistic should be avoided or neglected. However, when preaching widely, or to the people 'en masse', this discernment is not easily possible. The Āchāryas have said therefore, "preaching means a risk!"

11 The preachers of Kṛṣṇa consciousness will naturally be of different levels of devotional advancement. In a general sense, a preacher may be referred to as a teacher or a guide, as in the sense here; but the criteria of 'capacity' and 'empowerment' regarding the preacher's ability to deeply touch and convert souls to Kṛṣṇa consciousness, primarily refers to the higher level devotee and specifically empowered soul, the Āchārya, Spiritual Master.

Chapter Ten

The Horizon of Infinity

'To Catch the Moon...'

Devotee: It says in śāstra (scripture) that by a moment's association with a pure devotee one can attain all perfection.
Śrīla Śrīdhar Mahārāj: Yes. But 'perfection' in the Infinite is a relative term. When Kṛṣṇa is by the side of Rādhārāṇī, He is Svayam Bhagavān, that is, the fullest Kṛṣṇa, the most perfect Kṛṣṇa. But then there is prābhava-vikāsa and prābhava-vilāsa – Kṛṣṇa of different types, different aspects.[1] So, there is gradation in Kṛṣṇa also, what to speak of devotees and human beings. In everything, gradation is there. We are limited beings, so we are encouraged: "Search! Try to catch the Infinite as much as you can." In this way we are encouraged to see in the Āchārya, the highest teacher-ship.

But what is our capacity? We may try to our utmost to see in this way, but how much can we extend ourselves? Still, we are encouraged, "Whatever you can see, whatever you can conceive, as the Absolute, go forward with this consciousness. When you will reach to that point, there you will find something more, and from there, again go forward…" Just as we may think the sun is very near, but if we begin our journey towards it, we will find, "O, I thought, I conceived that it was here, but there is more. I must go further" and again, "still further"!

It is like a child who wants to 'catch the moon'. His father says, "The moon is nearby, I am getting it for you, my boy, don't cry." In this way, always the encouragement is given in our search, "It is very near."

Infinite Horizons

The truth is given, it is revealed, by instalments. Just as in education, the fullest encouragement should be given to the child to finish his studies in his present school, and when he has done so, there is further education, in the college. He is encouraged to collect all of his energy and to utilise it in his present point of progress, and then to go forward. And there is no end to this journey, back to our Lord, back to Home. At each stage of advancement, one will feel encouraged, but, at the same time, as much progress as he makes, so much he will be desperate, and feel disappointment: "I am not getting anything – it is so sweet, so sweet, I cannot taste even a drop."

Mahāprabhu Himself said, to His devotees, *na prema-gandho 'sti darāpi me harau* – "My dear friends, I have not the slightest scent of love of Godhead within My heart…" (*Śrī Chaitanya-charitāmṛta: Madhya-līlā, 2.45*). As much as souls will advance, as much as they are conscious of the Infinite, so much they think themselves as having nothing. They think themselves infinitesimal: "The Infinite is so big!!" The more they make progress, the more they find it is further, it is more: "O, the

'Infinite' – *this* is what it means, it is immense… I did not know that the Infinite is so vast, it has no 'circumference'! The Centre has no circumference, but it is everywhere!"

Devotee: So this process, this progress, it is going on eternally?

Śrīla Śrīdhar Mahārāj: Yes, it is always going on. But the Infinite is the lake of nectar, ocean of nectar, and so in relation to Him, there is no possibility of any loss. There is no possibility of being a loser, that "I will never be able to reach to the extremity, to the end, of this, so I will be lost." No! Because it is always more tasteful, more energy-giving, more hope-giving, and so encouraging, one cannot live without it. The soul feels he has not attained anything, but still he cannot stop his journey, and he is sure to go on, more and more. That is the nature of the path.[2]

Approval of the Inner Heart

The sweetness of this journey also is of infinite character. As much sweetness as the soul tastes, he wants more. In this way, everything, every aspect in relation to the Infinite, is infinite. That is Vaikuṇṭha. 'Kuṇṭha' means 'limit', so 'Vai-kuṇṭha' mean limitless, unlimited.[3] From the narrow, selfish conception of life we are to merge into the wider conception of the universal flow. We may think that by doing so we will lose our position, but, rather, we are in the process of acquiring a higher position. So we must proceed in this way, we must go further, go higher. This means to surrender, to 'die to live'. In this process we will feel that as much as we are eliminating, that we are 'losing' our previous position, so much we are making progress. Progress means to always go forward, to move ahead – the higher taste is there, and we get more and more life. So, we have to 'die to live', and death, so-called death, is encouraged by the gain of more vitality, more life. We can feel it – the more we 'die', the more we live – so we can't leave this campaign, can't abandon it, because the taste, the inner feeling is there. In this way all mundane attachments are naturally, gradually, eliminated:

viṣayā vinivartante
nirāhārasya dehinaḥ
rasa-varjaṁ raso 'py asya
paraṁ dṛṣṭvā nivartate
(Śrīmad Bhagavad-gītā: 2.59)

"The embodied being may renounce the sense objects but the taste for them remains. But that, too, vanishes for the man of wisdom"

In this way the experience of higher taste, higher ecstasy, encourages us to go further.

bhaktiḥ pareśānubhavo viraktir
anyatra chaiṣa trika eka-kālaḥ
prapadyamānasya yathāśnataḥ syus
tuṣṭiḥ puṣṭiḥ kṣud-apāyo 'nu-ghāsam
(*Śrīmad Bhāgavatam: 11.2.42*)[4]

"Devotion, direct experience of the Supreme Lord, and detachment from other things – these three occur simultaneously for one who has taken shelter of the Supreme Personality of Godhead, in the same way that pleasure, nourishment and relief from hunger come simultaneously and increasingly, with each bite, for a person engaged in eating."

'Viraktir' means abnegation, our devaluation of something, and to leave it behind; and 'pareśānubhavo' means that in front of us there is something of higher value, and the conception of a higher gain through that. In other words, what we leave behind us is of a lesser value, and what we gain, that is more valuable. 'Bhaktiḥ pareśānubhavo' means progress and some experience of gain – to lose the present stale position and to gain what is better, new, and encouraging, and to accept that. Progress means elimination and acceptance – acceptance of the higher, and elimination of the lower. And we ourselves will stand as witness and guarantee of that – hṛdayena-abhyanujñāto, our hearts' approval is there, to give us guarantee: "Go further!"

Existence Fulfilled

Devotee: So many of us aspiring Vaiṣṇavas, devotees, have started on the path, the long journey back towards Kṛṣṇa, but somehow we are checked in our progress. So, how do we continue in this journey?

Śrīla Śrīdhar Mahārāj: Everyone is trying to get more happiness, pleasure, but many are failing. Then what should we do? Should we not try to get pleasure? All are pleasure-hunting. Every point of existence, including trees, creepers, animals, men, women, everything in this world, all are searching for happiness, but we see that apparently many are failing. Then, should we stop this search? Can we even do so? We cannot. The urge to get greater happiness is a constant thing, we cannot leave it. It is even in the stone and in the fossil, but there it is covered.

The very nature of existence itself, is to search for pleasure, sukha, and this cannot be eliminated. All and any existence cannot be devoid of this tendency of searching for pleasure, for self-satisfaction. It is inherent, the most universal thing. As the very substance is existing, so is its tendency to get happiness in the way of freedom, knowledge, love – in any way, the tendency to progress in this direction is its inherent quality. It cannot be avoided. Even what one won't do by his voluntary will, he will be forced to do, to travel in that direction.

svabhāva-jena kaunteya,
nibaddhaḥ svena karmaṇā
kartuṁ nechchhasi yan mohāt,
kariṣyasy avaśo 'pi tat
(Śrīmad Bhagavad-gītā: 18.60)

"O Kaunteya, being bound by the duty born of your nature, that very action which out of delusion you are now avoiding, will be inevitably executed by you."

Material nature will force one to select that course born of his nature, and to always go forward – *prakṛti-sthāni karṣati (Śrīmad Bhagavad-gītā: 15.7)*. The environment will force every atom to move ahead, to progress.[5] Temporarily, we may think "I won't do that" – but that cannot be, it is not the real nature of things.

So, nature will not allow you to stop, idle. Sometimes, however, while in this process, in this progression, to take a rest is necessary, so it may be seen that at that time, the 'negative aspect' may come and say, "now take rest." But, that rest is also part of the progress. The Mahā-bhāgavata devotee is always engaged in the service of Kṛṣṇa, so when he is sleeping, that is also for the service of the Lord. He is taking rest so that with more energy he can serve; his sleep is also counted in the service.

Necessity's Gain

Devotee: When a devotee attempts to preach in the Western countries, or in any dangerous situation, does he or she get more protection from Mahāprabhu?

Śrīla Śrīdhar Mahārāj: Of course, and that will be according to their sincerity, their need, and their purity of purpose that they are preaching for Mahāprabhu and not for their own name and fame or any other acquisition. And there is preaching of different kinds, of different phases. There is preaching in the primary stage, and there the preachers may be many, but there is also preaching in higher stages, just as there are many primary schools, but higher education colleges are fewer.[6]

Devotee: If a devotee begins his journey to Kṛṣṇa, but he stops for some reason, is that due to his past karma or is it due to offences committed while performing devotional service?

Śrīla Śrīdhar Mahārāj: It may be.[7] However, it is difficult to have the proper conception about what may be the cause of that hindrance, that bad karma, because where the intensity of hankering for Kṛṣṇa is great, always in the retinue of that, the impression will come in the devotee that, "I have bad karma, bad luck." It is there in the highest position also.

There devotees will think, "I have bad luck." Rādhārāṇī Herself says, "It is my durdaiva-vilāsa, it is only the fruit of my bad karma that I am not getting union with Kṛṣṇa, that He has left Me. Kṛṣṇa is not to be blamed, He is full in all attributes, He is all right, but something is responsible for this separation. What is that? It is my bad luck."

So this feeling is always there in the devotee, and it manifests in different ways, even to the highest level. But that feeling of separation from the Lord is also another type of union with Him, 'union-in-separation'. By feeling in want, feeling such urgent necessity, it is a kind of gain. Earnest necessity for a thing which is not easily attained, that is a gain.

Devotee: But sometimes we see that a devotee loses the desire to attain Kṛṣṇa…

Śrīla Śrīdhar Mahārāj: That is dangerous. Hunger is a sign of good health – and not to have hunger, it is a sign of bad health!

Endnotes to Chapter 10

1 'Expansions' of Svayam Bhagavān Kṛṣṇa for different Pastimes.

2 The nature of the spiritual journey, and the experience of the seeker who is traveling it. That of ever approaching his goal, the Lord, but apparently never arriving there, as Śrīla Śrīdhar Mahārāj describes here, is one which, within the scope of their own theologies, is shared by other theistic faith-traditions. Jesuit theologian Karl Rahner (1904–1984) wrote about God as the 'Infinite Horizon', Whom one is always approaching but can never reach.

In the writings of the Cappadocian Father, St. Gregory of Nyssa, (335–395), this is also a recurring theme. As God is infinite in all ways, he says, consequently our drawing closer to Him is going to be an infinite journey, it will continue for all eternity. (He derives this from *St. Paul's Epistle to the Philippians* (3:13), that the sincere seeker must always be "straining forward to what lies ahead.") Gregory writes in his text, *On Perfection*: "Let us change in such a way that we may constantly evolve towards what is better, being transformed from glory to glory and from perfection to perfection, and thus always improving, ever becoming more perfect by daily growth and never arriving at any minute of perfection, but that perfection consists in our never stopping, and our growth being good."

Again, this theme is notable in the writings of the Christian Mystics of the late medieval period. St. John of the Cross (1542–1591) describes in *The Ascent of Mount Carmel*, how the soul rises up towards God, being stripped of all its earthly attachments so it can become 'empty' in order to be able to be filled with God's love. His expression here is 'nada, nada, nada', that is, 'nothing'. By this He does not mean that the soul is 'nothing', or that God is nothing – unless taken in the sense that He is 'no thing', that is to say, no thing of which one may have any experience through conditioned consciousness – but in the sense of the expression from Indian philosophy, 'neti, neti, neti', that is, 'not this, not this, not this'. In other words, God is always more, is higher, is greater, and indeed is sweeter, than is possible for the conditioned soul to conceive.

There are many other savants who could be cited in this regard. In Islam, particularly the Sufi tradition, there are many beautiful texts, poems and teachings on the states and stages of God-awakening. For example, Attar's *Conference of the Birds*; Ibn Arabi's *The Treatise on Being*; Jalaluddin Rumi's *Mathnawi*; Shabistari's *The Secret Rose Garden*, etc…

In Islam, of course, Allah, or God, always remains the great 'Unknown and Unknowable'. The Vaiṣṇava tradition, however, asserts that God can be 'known' – if He chooses to reveal Himself.

Once in a public meeting, Śrīla Śrīdhar Mahārāj was challenged by a gentleman, "If the infinitesimal soul can know the Infinite God, then He is not Infinite."

Śrīla Śrīdhar Mahārāj replied, "If the Infinite cannot reveal Himself to the finite, then He is not infinite!"

But the 'knowing' of God by the soul, is of a different order than what is generally understood as 'knowledge' – intellectual knowledge, or any kind of information, data-gathering, etc. Even in the mundane world, when we say that two people 'know each other', though it certainly includes such data – the persons' various tastes, proclivities, their name, address, and so on – it means something much more than this. It is a kind of knowing of the 'essence' of the other, at least touching it, in a point. So, in relation to the Absolute, mystics over the Ages have tried to convey their experience of God in words, and due to the ultimate inadequacy of such words, often poetry is the medium they use to express it.

The Sufi saints and philosophers sing of the passionate love of the soul for God, of the lover for the Beloved. Oxford scholar and spiritual seeker Andrew Harvey in his lecture series on Jalaluddin Rumi, entitled *Song of the Sun*, says: "Our modern addictions to reason, and the games of irony and control, have drained our psyches and souls of the heart-blood that keeps life abundant and miraculous, and the Sufi-lovers pump back that blood into us … the passion of the long Sufi tradition witnesses to the always-shattering glory of the Beloved and to the splendour of the journey towards Him, and that restores to us the greatness of our real life, its vast capacity for suffering and joy, the measureless growth of the spirit that we are capable of if we let ourselves be possessed and devoured by divine love, whatever path we are on."

Here, as an example, is one of Rumi's poems on the revelations and illuminations, intense, and sometimes bewildering, experienced in the second stage of the 'unfolding of the rose' in which the soul has glimpses and foretastes of the Union with God which will be fully experienced in later stages. Rumi says to the Lord: "You are my soul, my universe; what do I have to do with the soul and the universe? For me, You are ever-flowing treasure. What do I have to do with profit or loss? One minute I am the friend of the wine, another the friend of Him Who burns me. I have come to this age of ruins, so what do I have to do with time's melodrama? I am terrified by the whole world, I am sprung free of the whole world, I am neither hidden nor apparent, what do I have to do with existence, or space, I am drunk on union with You, I need and want and care about no one else. Since I am Your prey, what do I care about fate's bow and its arrows? I live at the bottom of the stream, why would I go looking for water? What could or would I say about this stream that flows and flows? I have given up existence, why go on staggering under the burden of this mountain? And since the wolf is my shepherd, why put up with the pretensions of the shepherd? What abandon, what drunkenness, You hold the cup in Your hand, and blessed is the place You are, and glorious to the eye of the heart. Each atom by Your grace is a universe, each drop of water a soul, and no one who has ever had a sign from You need worry again about name or sign. To find the place of splendour at the bottom of the sea of truths, you have to dive, dive head-first, what do I have to do with feet that scurry? With the sword of the one God, You have hacked a path for us, You have stolen all my clothes, what will I give to the toll-man? From Your beauty ablaze like the Sun, from the curls of Your hair, my heart has become ecstatic. O my soul, hand me this brimming cup, do not weigh pain and misery, contemplate love, contemplate friendship, do not mull over tyranny and neglect, think of all who have their eyes fixed on You. Surname all grief 'grace', transmute pain and anguish into joy, and ask from joy all happiness, all security, all peace – demand that security, that peace, demand them, choose the company of those withdrawn in love, listen to those who open a path to You – listen, and don't say a word."

If God can be 'known' at all, then, this can only be through love. Meister Eckhart, 14th century Dominican theologian famously said, "God can only be captured by love – by intellect, never." This 'capturing' of the Supreme Lord through love, cannot be seen through a better example than that in the Vaiṣṇava tradition of Mother Yaśodā's literally capturing her mischievous little boy, Kṛṣṇa – the Supreme Personality of Godhead – apparently with a cord, but actually with her pure love (see *Śrīmad Bhāgavatam: 10.14*).

We should also note here, on the subject of the souls' search for God being endless, that according to Vaiṣṇava teachings, the perfection of liberation in relation to the Supreme Lord, means the soul's realisation of its eternal serving-form: *muktir hitvānyathā-rūpaṁ svarūpeṇa vyavasthitiḥ*. Liberation is the permanent situation of the form of the living entity after he gives up the changeable gross and subtle material bodies." *(Śrīmad Bhāgavatam: 2.10.6)*. Even after attainment of this stage however – being situated in one's eternal serving mood manifesting through one of the five primary rasas, or relationships, of śānta (peaceful, neutral), dāsya (service), sakhya (friendship), vātsalya (parental), and mādhurya (conjugal) – this attainment, though the final 'state' of the soul, is not a 'static' position, for the service rendered from this position increases, by divine inspiration, in depth of love and affection, in quality and quantity, and this progression, again, has no end.

3 Śrīla A.C. Bhaktivedānta Swāmī Prabhupāda, in his writings renders 'Vaikuṇṭha' as 'free from suffering'. But both versions may be seen as amounting to the same meaning, because all suffering occurs on account of limitations, in one form or another.

4 In this famous verse of *Śrīmad Bhāgavatam*, Śrī Kavi, the leader of the Nava-yogendras, the nine Yogendra saints, instructs Mahārāj Nimi in the glories of devotional service. This history is being recounted by Devarṣi Nārada, to Vasudev, the father of Lord Kṛṣṇa.

5 It is the inherent law of nature that everything, under the influence of time ('kāla'), even if it may appear inert, like stone or wood, is actually constantly moving and changing, as has been shown by modern atomic physics. What appears to be a 'solid' table today, in a thousand or a million years time, will be a pile of dust, and then recycled into yet another form. In the material world, the effect of this constant change must be deterioration. But Śrīla Śrīdhar Mahārāj is here using the word 'progress' simply to mean the 'process of constant evolution, development'. In the case of the individual person, though the natural tendency of the soul is always to progress in a positive direction, towards the light, towards God, the effects of the lower modes of material nature are such that, as Śrīla Śrīdhar Mahārāj elsewhere points out, because of the minute free-will of the conditioned soul, sometimes "progress can also be in a wrong direction." (In *Bhagavad-gītā*, Chapter 16, Lord Kṛṣṇa gives a vivid description of the nature and effects of this.)

6 Regarding the soul's progress towards the 'infinite horizon' of God, we may also note here the difference between what may be called 'states' and 'stages' in the spiritual life. These are known to

the spiritual traditions, and have more recently been recognised and analysed by modern transpersonal psychology. The distinction between states and stages is important because it can explain to some extent the apparent discrepancy sometimes found between teaching, and behaviour, in regards to spiritual mentors – the subject of not a little controversy. Spiritual 'states' may be experienced by a person at any 'stage' of spiritual growth, from childhood onwards, but they are temporary 'peak' experiences which, while they may be subjectively profound, even life-changing, are distinct from 'stages', which are (relatively) permanent, stable plateaus of growth which the soul progressively attains on its journey, each stage including but transcending the previous one. Ideally, states and stages should develop in sync, in a balanced individual.

[7] i.e. presumably, it may be due to either, or both, of the reasons mentioned by the questioner.

Chapter Eleven

The Slightest Touch

A Peculiar Position

Śrīla Śrīdhar Mahārāj: The Lord is everywhere, but we need to have the real eye to see Him. He is everywhere, there is no place where He is not present – yet, He is 'nowhere'! He says: "I am everywhere; at the same time, I am nowhere! Everything is in Me; nothing is in Me, Arjuna! Try to understand My peculiar position, Who I am!"

mayā tatam idaṁ sarvaṁ
jagad avyakta-mūrtinā
mat-sthāni sarva-bhūtāni
na chāhaṁ teṣv avasthitaḥ
(Śrīmad Bhagavad-gītā: 9.4)

"This entire universe is pervaded by Me in My un-manifest form, and all beings are situated in Me; yet I am not in them."

na cha mat-sthāni bhūtāni
paśya me yogam aiśvaram
bhūta-bhṛn na cha bhūta-stho
mamātmā bhūta-bhāvanaḥ
(Śrīmad Bhagavad-gītā: 9.5)

"Again, they are not in Me. Behold My supreme mystical power of inconceivable oneness and difference (achintya-bhedābheda). I am the mainstay and origin of all beings, but I am not in them."

Just as in the case of the material elements, the ether is present everywhere, and everything is in it, but still, the other elements are not ether, and ether is not them. It is something like that. Kṛṣṇa says:

yathā mahānti bhūtāni
bhūteṣūchchāvacheṣv anu
praviṣṭāny apraviṣṭāni
tathā teṣu na teṣv aham
(Śrīmad Bhāgavatam: 2.9.35)

"O Brahmā, please know that the universal elements enter into the cosmos and at the same time do not enter into the cosmos; similarly, I Myself also exist within everything created, and at the same time I am outside of everything."

This is simultaneous oneness and difference, or 'distinction' and 'non-distinction'. Mahāprabhu named it, 'achintya-bheda-abheda': inconceivably, there is something common, and something different, between one thing and another. This is the general characteristic of everything.

One Step Below

The direct connection with the Lord, that is not possible for us at present, so our Guru Mahārāj, Śrīla Bhakti Siddhānta Saraswatī Ṭhākur, told us: "Think that you are one step lower. Don't try to have direct connection with Him. Your guru, he is there, in direct connection with Him, and you are just below, on the step below, and from there you are trying to carry out his order."

That advice was a great help to me. It is a peaceful position because, if directly, from the 'front', you will be always searching, very keenly searching for the Lord, but not finding Him, you will be unsatisfied, "O, it is not possible to find Him." That is very troublesome. But rather from behind, from the 'second step', that is peaceful: to go on searching, according to your guru's order, thinking that, "I am not in direct connection with the Lord, but my guru is in direct connection with Him, and according to his advice I am going on with service, with faith that the Lord is there." That is a peaceful attitude, and a safe position, and it is also recommended by both śāstra (scriptures) and sādhu (saints). So, take that position; don't try to stand in direct connection with the Lord, but a little indirect.

Indestructible Connection

Kuntī Devī wanted unfavourable circumstances, materially. She considered that as favourable for her relationship with the Lord, for divya-darśan, for His real connection. Generally, our calculation may be for favourable circumstances, but she invited danger in life, for when we are helpless, disappointed, under pressure from every direction, naturally our search for a solution will go towards the Lord. Our self-forgetfulness, our surrender, will be increased. So, such adverse circumstances may be favourable for us for our spiritual life.

In any case, once coming in connection with Kṛṣṇa, no destruction can come to a person – na vinaśyati[1]. Any connection, a slightest connection, with Him – *tatra svalpa sambandha* – that will save one, definitely, because such connection is invulnerable to the extreme. Nothing can oppose, crush, or destroy it. It is of such quality. Even a connection with Vaikuṇṭha, or even with

Brahma, or Paramātmā, that also cannot be destroyed.[2] The Absolute is such. None can stand, fighting against Him. Ultimately He will conquer everything – all others will have to retire, they cannot stand in competition with Him.[3]

māṁ hi pārtha vyapāśritya
ye 'pi syuḥ pāpa-yonayaḥ
striyo vaiśyās tathāśūdrās
te 'pi yānti parāṁ gatim
(Bhagavad-gītā: 9.32)

"O son of Pṛthā, those who take shelter in Me, though they be of lower birth, women, merchants, or labourers, attain the Supreme destination."

If any 'mal'-thing has a connection with Him, that also is delivered, and goes to Him. Those without such connection, will be finished through reaction,[4] but in His connection, there is no reaction.

Don't Deceive Yourself

What does it mean, 'to see Kṛṣṇa'? There was a man who lived on the banks of the Ganges here in Nabadwīp about forty years ago.[5] One day he approached me and said, "I have seen Kṛṣṇa!"

I told him, "To do so is not such a cheap thing. Don't say such to me – go to some other person."

"No, no, I have seen Him, and not only have I seen Him, but I have shown Him to many others here." He went on with this kind of mad talk.

I told him, "We have made some study, we have got some understanding about what is Kṛṣṇa, and how to see Him, what are the signs or symptoms of that, and all such things – so do not believe that like any ordinary person I shall follow you, to 'see' Kṛṣṇa!"

"But it is true, I showed Him to so many."

I told him, "Yes, you might have seen some monkeys…[6] Kṛṣṇa is not so cheap, it is not that He will just come, so easily, to your physical eyes." I spoke to him in this way.

Then that gentleman went away. When he came again, with the same story, I told him: "Why are you deceiving yourself? Do you know Who is Kṛṣṇa, and who can see Him? And after seeing Him, what will be the condition of that person? Do you have any knowledge, some general knowledge about this? You yourself know how you are troubled by lust, anger, greed, and so many such things which are within you; and you say you are a brāhmaṇa's son, and yet with that fortunate human birth, you are wasting it. You are deceiving others, and yourself. Don't deceive yourself."

This created some impression in him, and after thinking about it for some days, he left everything – he took off his female dress, and cut off his long hair[7] – and he came back: "Yes, what you have said, it is true. I am still a slave of my senses. How can I get Kṛṣṇa so easily?"

He requested me for dīkṣā, initiation, but one of my god-brothers was here at that time, and he gave caution: "Don't do so; he is a hypocrite. Today he has come to you, tomorrow or another day he will run to some other person, some other clan. Don't believe him." So, I avoided that.

Kṛṣṇa is not so easy to be seen or to be attained, to be 'caught within the fist'. He is everywhere, and He is nowhere – everything is in Him, and nothing is in Him, at the same time.[8] We must always be conscious of this. So, the search for Kṛṣṇa, it is with this background.

No Demand

The higher devotees feel that even desiring to see the Lord is also some kind of 'enjoyment'. They say, "No, no, we won't disturb His sweet will. Whenever He likes, He may call for us, then we shall get the chance to see Him, otherwise not. We want Kṛṣṇa, but not to order Him, 'O Kṛṣṇa, come and stand before us, we want to see You for our satisfaction.'" This demand is a kind of imposition by our exploiting nature. The devotees do not want that for the satisfaction of their eye, or their inner hankering, the Lord has to come and show Himself. This is not the conception of the higher devotees; they do not allow these thoughts to enter. Rather, they think, "Whenever Kṛṣṇa feels the necessity, He will call for me; then I shall have the chance of seeing Him." They never desire Kṛṣṇa to serve them, supply them, or give them darśan of Himself.

To impose our whim on the Lord is not service proper. Whatever Kṛṣṇa likes, He may do. We shall consider ourselves fortunate if we are given a chance to supply whatever is necessary for His service. We are to place ourselves fully at the disposal of that Supreme Autocrat Who is to command us, to order us, and never to carry out any order from us. But, it is the Lord's nature, that He is eager to supply everything for His devotees:

ananyāś chintayanto māṁ
ye janāḥ paryupāsate
teṣāṁ nityābhiyuktānāṁ
yoga-kṣemaṁ vahāmy aham
(Śrīmad Bhagavad-gītā: 9.22)

"I bear the responsibility of acquiring and protecting the necessities of My fully dependent devotees who are always absorbed in thought of Me, and who worship Me in every way."

Still, devotees of higher realisation do not prefer Kṛṣṇa to supply them with anything, or serve them in any way. Their ananya-bhakti, their purest devotion, is of this quality. They sincerely feel, "He is our Lord, through faith. We don't want to 'see' Him in order to satisfy our lower faculties, that He does indeed 'exist'. We have no capacity to see Him."

A 'lower kind of faith' means trying to become the subject, and making Him the object. A higher kind of faith, a more intense faith, proves that He is the Original Subjective Cause of everything.

A Place in the Harmony

How is one to maintain his position within the current of Kṛṣṇa consciousness? That we must know. That current is always flowing, and to maintain one's position within it, requires some force, some energy. The attempt to maintain oneself may apparently seem to be something passive, or static, it may appear that in relation to the Infinite, 'no progress is progress', but in fact it requires effort, it is dynamic.[9] And to maintain one's position in unfavourable circumstances, is not very easy. But to feel separation from the Lord, to feel pain in the striving for harmony, that "I am not having any place in the sweet harmony of relations with Him" – that is more intense than to feel, "I have got Him."

It is a very peculiar thing. The greatest necessity for Him – that necessity is He, Himself. In this sense, to approach Him, to come to Him, is to get Him.[10]

I once delivered a lecture at a meeting in Madras (Chennai) where some scholars of the Madhva school had made arrangement to honour the birthday of Madhva Āchārya.[11] They made me the President at the meeting, and Nāgarāj Sharma, a Professor of the Madhva school, was to deliver lectures there. At the beginning of the meeting I gave some introductory talk, and there I mentioned about Mahāprabhu's teaching:

tṛṇād api sunīchena
taror iva sahiṣṇunā
amāninā mānadena
kīrtanīyaḥ sadā hariḥ
(Śikṣāṣṭakam: 3)

"One who is humbler than a blade of grass, more forbearing than a tree, who gives due honour to others without desiring it for himself, is qualified to always chant the Holy Name of Kṛṣṇa."

Then when Professor Sharma gave his lecture, I traced there a slight touch, a remark, that "To think one's own self to be meaner than a blade of grass, what is the achievement there? To think oneself to be very low, very mean – how can that be the means to attain the higher things?" I caught in his speech, a slight remark of this kind.

Afterwards, at the conclusion of the meeting, again I got the chance to speak; and I mentioned, "Who can see himself as small, as mean, is in the relativity of the Big. The jīva-soul can only think of himself as lowest of the lowest when he is having a real conception of the Infinite; as much as he can have some conception of the Infinite, he cannot but think himself, in comparison, as meanest of the mean."

Genuine realisation about the Lord is measured by this standard. What, and how much, can the soul see? Who sees himself as big, will see other things as small; but one who is really living in relation with the Infinite, cannot but feel himself as smallest of the small, meanest of the mean. That is the real criterion of our improvement on our journey towards consciousness of the Infinite, towards Him.

Endnotes to Chapter 11

[1] *Na vinasyati*: 'no destruction', from *Bhagavad-gītā*, 6.40:

> **(śrī-bhagavān uvācha):**
> **pārtha naiveha nāmutra, vināśas tasya vidyate**
> **na hi kalyāṇa-kṛt kaśchid, durgatiṁ tāta gachchhati**

Śrīla Śrīdhar Mahārāj often quoted the second line, *na hi kalyāṇa-kṛt kaśchid durgatiṁ tāta gachchhati*, as evidence of Lord Kṛṣṇa's mercy on the sincerely aspiring soul, that, "they will never meet destruction." The full translation of this verse appears in his rendition of *Bhagavad-gītā, Hidden Treasure of the Sweet Absolute*, as follows:

"The Supreme Lord said: 'O Arjuna, son of Kuntī, there is no loss for the unsuccessful yoga practitioner as he is not denied the happiness of the heavenly plane in this world, nor is he denied the chance of the fortune to see the Super-soul in the transcendental realm. This is so, O dear one, because a person who performs virtuous actions never suffers an ill fate.'"

Śrīla A.C. Bhaktivedānta Swāmī Prabhupāda renders this verse concisely in his *Bhagavad-gītā As It Is*:

The Blessed Lord said: "Son of Pṛthā, a transcendentalist engaged in auspicious activities does not meet with destruction either in this world or in the spiritual world; one who does good, My friend, is never overcome by evil."

Note: Śrīla Prabhupāda dedicates *Bhagavad-gītā As It Is* to Śrīla Baladev Vidhyābhūṣaṇa, who was a śikṣā disciple of Śrīla Viśvanātha Chakravartī Ṭhākur. Both of these Āchāryas made translations with commentary of *Śrī Gīta* entitled respectively

Śrī Gīta-bhuṣaṇa and *Sārārtha-Varṣiṇī-Ṭīkā*, with which Śrīla Prabhupāda was certainly familiar. Śrīla Chakravartī Ṭhākur's own translation of this verse renders into English:

"O son of Pṛthā, he does not meet destruction in this life or the next. One who has done the auspicious work of yoga does not meet an unfortunate end, a destination of suffering, O dear one."

2 **vadanti tat tattva-vidas**
tattvaṁ yaj jñānam advayam
brahmeti paramātmeti
bhagavān iti śabdyate
(Śrīmad Bhāgavatam: 1.2.11)

"Learned transcendentalists who know the Absolute Truth call this non-dual substance Brahman, Paramātmā, or Bhagavān."

God is realised in three phases: as all-pervading Brahman by the jñānīs; as all-permeating Paramātmā (Super-soul) by the yogīs; and as Bhagavān, the Supreme Personality of Godhead, by the devotees.

3 i.e. all other propositions about the purpose of life, and even all other existing conceptions of religion, and of God, will have no other option but retire before the all-attractive charm and beauty of Kṛṣṇa, and Kṛṣṇa consciousness.

4 They will be 'vanquished', they will have to go down on the karma-chakra, the wheel of karma, by having to suffer the fruits of their own action.

5 i.e. about 1945, four years after Śrīla Śrīdhar Mahārāj came to live in Kolerganj, Nabadwīp Dhām, the Holy Place of Śrī Chaitanya Mahāprabhu.

6 Śrīla Śrīdhar Mahārāj is saying, not without irony, "Yes, you might have seen, perhaps, some monkeys playing in the distance and deluded yourself that you had seen the Pastimes of Kṛṣṇa!"

[7] Westerners, and/or newcomers to the path of Kṛṣṇa-bhakti, devotion to Kṛṣṇa, might be shocked to hear of such an extreme aberration of the path of devotional service – males adopting female dress, hair, ornaments and all such particulars and imagining themselves thus as gopīs, female milkmaids, in love with Kṛṣṇa. But such groups have existed, particularly since the time of Śrī Chaitanya Mahāprabhu, claiming to be true followers of His teachings. They are however, understood as sahajiyās or imitationists by the actual disciples of Lord Chaitanya, and their many moral misconducts, abhorrent to even law-abiding secular folk, had until the revival of Chaitanya-bhakti by Śrīla Bhakti Vinod Ṭhākur (1838–1914), tarnished the reputation of Gauḍīya Vaiṣṇavism in society.

Their misunderstanding is based on the mixing of spiritual conception with the mundane – taking Kṛṣṇa-prema, love of Kṛṣṇa, to be the same as kāma, material lust, and acting in that way. This was totally repudiated by Śrīla Bhakti Vinod Ṭhākur in his writings, and then vigorously opposed, and philosophically defeated, by his illustrious son and disciple, Śrīla Bhakti Siddhānta Saraswatī Ṭhākur (1874–1936), the founder of Śrī Gauḍīya Maṭh.

Śrīla Śrīdhar Mahārāj also, is renowned for his strict adherence to the true line of Śrī Chaitanyadev and rejection of all such sahjiyā notions, in theory and practice. (There were thirteen such sects as delineated by Śrīla Bhakti Siddhānta Saraswatī: āula, bāula, sakhībheki, etc. One such sect, kartābhaja, is said to have up to five million followers in the early 1900s!)

[8] *Bhagavad-gītā*, 9.4–5 as quoted earlier.

[9] Apparently, 'no progress is progress'. By analogy, it is something like a person, who when in the current of a river, by various movements of their limbs, though such movements are apparently slight, is able to stay afloat and can avoid being drawn to either bank and deposited thereupon; indeed, they can keep themselves in a

forward motion and direction. It may appear to the casual observer that the 'floater' is not really 'doing' anything, but in fact they are engaged in a very definite, though subtle movement.

In the very beginning of devotional practising life, acting for Kṛṣṇa, though it is the constitutional position of the soul, sometimes feels to the practitioner very difficult because for life times the conditioned soul has been acting for his 'self-interest' (exploitation). This is like the difficulty of cranking an engine to get it started. When it is running, then the business is to 'maintain' the motion, and that is by certain actions that do not outwardly appear very 'dynamic' – applying a little oil here and there, adjusting certain parts, etc. – but those actions are very significant, they protect the machine from breaking down. In devotional terms, these 'maintenance activities' are the regular activities of sādhana-bhakti (devotional practising life), but most particularly, a certain vigilance – one has to protect the newly-sprouted, delicate plant of devotion (bhakti-lata) from various 'weeds' which will choke it, or take energy meant to nourish it, for their own interest. 'Weeds', for example, would be the over-collecting of money or material assets (under the guise of spiritual service), too much interest in worldly affairs, or associating with materialists or 'impersonalists'. A fuller delineation of this may be found in Śrīla Rūpa Goswāmī's text *Upadeśāmṛta, Nectar of Instruction*. All in all, the activities of a devotee, one engaged in bhakti-yoga, may not appear very great, or significant, to the mundane vision, as compared for example to those of the siddha-yogi, who performs many penances, austerities, and even mystic feats which appear impressive to people in general – but because the aim of the devotee is, through guru and Vaiṣṇava, to please the Lord, and the satisfaction of the Lord is the real purpose of life, their activities are in reality, much the greater.

[10] Feelings of separation from the Lord can, in fact, be more powerful than feeling His presence. As it is said, 'absence makes the heart grow fonder' – separation from the Lord, though apparently extremely painful, produces in the soul a deeper and more intense

ecstasy of union. This kind of worship of Kṛṣṇa in separation, was both taught and demonstrated by Śrī Chaitanya Mahāprabhu as the highest and most desirable attainment in Kṛṣṇa consciousness. To cultivate Kṛṣṇa consciousness in the mood of 'separation', even from the beginning stages of spiritual practice, is also the safe way to avoid the path of imitationism (prākṛta-sahajiyā-vāda), as the previous story of the 'monkey-seer' illustrates!

The principle that the intense desire for the Lord is, itself, a manifestation of Him, has been expressed by savants of different theistic faith traditions. St. Gregory of Nyssa (335–395) wrote: "To find God, is to seek Him unceasingly. Here, indeed, to seek is not one thing, and to find, another…"

St. Catherine of Siena (1347–1380), wrote in her *Dialogues*: "You are a mystery as deep as the sea; the more I search, the more I find, and the more I find, the more I search for You. But I can never be satisfied; what I receive will ever leave me desiring more. When You fill my soul I have an even greater hunger, and I grow more famished for Your light."

[11] Śrīla Madhva Āchārya (1238–1317), great Vaiṣṇava, devotee of Kṛṣṇa. He is a renowned Āchārya representing the lineage originating from Lord Brahmā, one of the four recognised Vaiṣṇava sampradāyas (lineages). Śrī Chaitanya Mahāprabhu, showing the example of an ideal devotee, took His dīkṣa, initiation, from Śrī Īśvara Purī in the Madhva line. (Some say He did so because, among the Vaiṣṇava lineages, Śrī Madhva Āchārya with his suddha-dvaita [pure dualism] teaching, most distinctly expressed that aspect of the jīva-souls as being different, or distinct from the Supreme Lord – traditionally, Madhva is depicted holding his right hand aloft with forefinger and second finger extended to emphasise this distinction.)

All Vaiṣṇava sampradāyas accept service to the Lord as the verity, and therefore oppose the idea of the soul and the Lord's 'absolute oneness' (kevalādvaita-vāda), the monism propounded by Śrī Śaṅkara Āchārya (788–820). Madhva fought with and defeated many Śaṅkarite scholars. His main Maṭh or monastery is in Udupi, Karnataka (South India), and the worship of Kṛṣṇa he propounded was that of 'Bāla-Kṛṣṇa', Kṛṣṇa as a young child – worship in the mood of vātsalya or parental affection. The followers in the Madhva line are known as tattvavādīs. Since Śrī Chaitanya Mahāprabhu, the lineage has been known as the Brahma-Madhva-Gauḍīya Sampradāya. (Gauḍīya from Gauḍa-deśa or Bengal where Mahāprabhu appeared). With the advent of Śrī Chaitanyadev the worship of Rādhā-Kṛṣṇa in the mood of conjugal love (mādhurya-rasa) manifested, and there are some other developments which Mahāprabhu brought to the lineage. Madhva Āchārya was a staunch and indomitable Vaiṣṇava, unwavering in his principles which were like 'lines carved on stone'. He gave a commentary on *Śrīmad Bhāgavatam*, but omitted Chapters 13 and 14 of Canto 10, in which the brahma-vimohana-līlā, the 'bewilderment of Lord Brahmā' by Kṛṣṇa in Vṛndāvan, is described – that is, how the founding father and original guru of the lineage, Lord Brahmā was so easily put into illusion by Kṛṣṇa! Śrīla Madhva Āchārya was also possessed of great physical strength; he is said to be an incarnation of Śrī Vāyu, the wind-god.

Chapter Twelve

The Strategy of our Search

Mahāprabhu's Samādhi

As much connection as we get with the Lord, so much our hankering for Him will be intensified. We will feel, "O, He is so good, so beautiful, so captivating, so charming!" – such will be the sign or symptom of the soul's development and proximity to Him. And the opposite, to think that "I have got Him", that will be like dreaming, we will think it to be an abnormal position or condition.

In *Śrī Chaitanya-charitāmṛta*, in the talks between Chaitanya Mahāprabhu and Rāmānanda Rāya, we find this verse:

ye kāle vā svapane, dekhinu vaṁśī-vadane,
sei kāle āilā dui vairi
'ānanda' āra 'madana', hari' nila mora mana,
dekhite nā pāinu netra bhari'

(Śrī Chaitanya-charitāmṛta: Madhya-līlā, 2.37)

"Whenever I had the chance to see Lord Kṛṣṇa's face and His flute, even in a dream, two enemies would appear before Me.

They were pleasure and Cupid, and since they took away My mind, I was not able to see the face of Kṛṣṇa to the full satisfaction of My eyes."

Mahāprabhu thought, "When I got Him in a dream, that was not normal, I was in an 'abnormal' position. He came and united with Me, that seems to Me to be like a dream…" This is a peculiar thing. When there is meeting, there is union, with the Lord, there is for the time being a wonderful experience of satisfaction – but that is not permanent, so Mahāprabhu says that meeting was like a 'dream'. But in the ocean of viraha, separation from the Lord, though apparently one is always hankering, unsatisfied, while others are enjoying with the Lord, still, when one is observing this from a distance, this position, 'second' position, can be more permanent, and that gives greater satisfaction. This was Mahāprabhu's experience in His 'dream'. Afterwards He is describing to the devotees how in His transcendental condition, samādhi, He was in Govardhan, and there are the gopīs, and Kṛṣṇa, and He is seeing how the gopīs are arranging, devising in different ways for Kṛṣṇa's service, and what is their mood, and how they are going to be united with Him.

Mahāprabhu said, "I was seeing all this with great pleasure… When I saw all these arrangements for the gopīs' union with Kṛṣṇa, I felt I was swimming in the innermost and purest type of pleasure." He felt Himself to be not in direct connection with Kṛṣṇa, but was observing from outside, as an onlooker, from one step further behind – and that had permanence and gave Him the fullest satisfaction.

Then Mahāprabhu told the devotees: "O, the beauty of their (gopīs') movements, the sweet sound of their ornaments, how beautiful it is, I was seeing it… At that time, you all took Me away from there, to this material world, by chanting the Name of Kṛṣṇa … by that kolāhala, by the noise of the sound of the Name of Kṛṣṇa, you drew My attention to this plane of affliction. You have made Me disappointed, you have taken Me away from that happy connection…" In His samādhi, as if in a 'dream' state, Mahāprabhu had this experience of Kṛṣṇa-līlā.[1]

Secret of Success

In this way, the soul's deeper experience of the Lord is 'indirect'. It is like a telescopic system: if something is very far away, and we want to see it directly, we cannot. It is only by seeing through many lenses, which have some apparent gap, some distance between them, and which stand between ourself and that for which we are looking, that we can have some idea about it.[2] Or, it is like the sun: we can see him from a particular distance, but if we want to see him from nearer we will be destroyed. Approaching towards him, we will be finished on the way.[3] So, we will adjust ourselves in this way, always to look from behind the guru and the Vaiṣṇava, and with this strategy we can have some experience about the Lord. This is the principle of service life: *tad dāsa-dāsa-dāsānudāsa aham dehi* – I am to serve the servant of the servant's servant, of the Lord, and not to approach Him directly.

The ideal of the followers of Mahāprabhu is Rādhā-dāsyam, submission to the greatest 'seer', Rādhārāṇī. Always behind Her – or, in other rasas, behind Kṛṣṇa – behind Him, or behind Her, from that position we are to have His sight. That is *yogaḥ karmasu kauśalam*[4] – the strategy, the 'trade-secret', the secret of success. It is the testing point to guide us.

Kṛṣṇa, Stealer of Hearts

Kṛṣṇa is everywhere, but we can't see Him! Everything is in Him, and He is everywhere, but we cannot see Him, He is 'lost' to us. A peculiar thing! But really, He is the existence of all existence, He is maintaining all existence, and He is behind, He is the foundation of all existence. And sometimes the Lord likes to play 'hide-and-seek' with the devotees; sometimes He comes clear, and sometimes He is vague. Whenever He is vague, the devotees begin to cry, "Where are You, my Lord? I don't feel You, I cannot see You. How can I continue my life? How can I live without You? You are so charming, so joyous, so fulfilling that I cannot live without Your connection."

But, because Kṛṣṇa is a 'thief', we have hope! 'Navanīta-chora' – 'chora' means thief. Kṛṣṇa is 'chora'. Chora, always stealing. To steal everything is His habit. His nature, His very existence, also, may be conceived in this way. Because a thief comes and goes stealthily, his activity is always undercover, unknown, stealthy – and when Kṛṣṇa comes, He comes as a thief.

When I was a student in Berhampore College, I went to hear a lecture from one gentleman, a Goswāmī, and I remember he said, "Because Kṛṣṇa is a thief, we have some hope. How? Because, we can invite to our house many big men,[5] but they may not have time to come – but a thief, even if we try to avoid him by erecting high walls, employing 'durwans',[6] and so on, still, uninvited, stealthily, he comes, and finishes his duty!"

Our nature is such, that we have erected within us many boundary walls so that none can enter, and even God cannot enter, but because Kṛṣṇa is a thief, He comes uninvited, enters our heart, and captures it. And that is our advantage. We may put up thousands of barriers to obstruct any entry, but a thief manages all these difficulties, these obstructions, oppositions, and still comes. As conditioned souls, our position is such that we are accustomed to have so many barriers in us to protect our exploitation, so that nothing shall disturb our exploiting business of different types. And so many barriers are there in us for 'renunciation', to protect that, also – but He does not care for all these blockades, He comes, and captures our heart. So it is our solace, that He is a thief, otherwise, we have no hope. All the barriers we have erected within us, to guard us, they are our samskāras,[7] gross and subtle, and they are the superstition of separatism, the knowledge and conception of separate interest from the Lord. But only because Kṛṣṇa is a thief, He does not care for any of these various barriers, He will come anyhow, and steal our heart.

Not a Doll of Imagination

Devotee: Guru Mahārāj, while preaching, sometimes people ask us, "Have you seen Kṛṣṇa? If you have not seen Kṛṣṇa, how can you preach about Him?"
Śrīla Śrīdhar Mahārāj: Is it very easy to see Kṛṣṇa? He is not a doll of my concoction, of my eternally forgetful nature. Who is Kṛṣṇa? Kṛṣṇa, the Kṛṣṇa conception, it is not such an easy thing. He is everywhere – and He is nowhere. When we are searching for Him, then we can take it that He is everywhere – this kind of thinking is also not eliminated – but rather, we have to think that He is 'nowhere', that is to say, we are encouraged to think He is there in the Guru and in the Vaiṣṇava.

So we are to try to see in this way, that, "To me, He is nowhere; but to my Guru He is everywhere." And that is also not just for the time being, but always He is above the head of my Guru. So, when I cannot have any direct vision of the Lord, if I try to see Him always in this way, on the head of my Guru, then He will come with him, to me. We are to mould ourselves in such a way, then we may have some real acquaintance with Him, with our Lord.

The Work of Yogamāyā [8]

In the verse where Mahāprabhu is describing His 'dream' of Kṛṣṇa (*ye kāle vā svapane...*) we see the work of Yogamāyā and the importance of serving the Lord through His 'paraphernalia'. Mahāprabhu said, "Just when Kṛṣṇa gave this sight to Me, two 'enemies' came to capture Me: ānanda, some sort of ecstatic feeling, and madana (cupid), my heart was captured by an unprecedented pleasure, inestimable pleasure. They got the upper hand and disturbed Me, disturbed My perception of Him. Because of these two feelings – ānanda-madana-mohana – at that moment I could not have any proper estimation of Him, *Hari' nila mora mana*. But, if in the future I get such a chance to see Kṛṣṇa, then I shall try to propitiate time, so that he may not pass but will stand still! Time's coming and going is like lightning, he never stays, so when I try to see Him, to see Kṛṣṇa – the moment has already passed. But if I can 'fix' time, if I can propitiate, if I can satisfy him, then he will stay, for some time, and I will be able to have a perception of Him, of my Lord." This is the work of Yogamāyā.

In the spiritual world, there is 'relativity' in the Absolute, in the Pastimes of the Lord, and all the arrangements for the service of the Lord are the work of Yogamāyā. Just as, when a king is to come to a certain place, everything depends mainly on his paraphernalia and the arrangements, and not so much on him. His associates will say, "Yes, you can go there, it is quite safe, and you will be welcomed, given reception with dignity by them." All such arrangements and paraphernalia are very important, they are indispensable, and intrinsic, in the Pastimes, and they are under the management of Yogamāyā. As Kṛṣṇa is infinite, His paraphernalia is also infinite. A 'king' means, he has a lot of paraphernalia, high paraphernalia, and Yogamāyā manages it. As Mahāprabhu prayed that for Kṛṣṇa's connection, He would propitiate time, so in our service, we shall try to satisfy the paraphernalia of the Lord.

Captured By Love

Kṛṣṇa says, "Though I am independent, still, practically, I am dependent on, I am obliged to My devotees who have left everything for Me."

ahaṁ bhakta-parādhīno
hy asvatantra iva dvija
sādhubhir grasta-hṛdayo
bhaktair bhakta-jana-priyaḥ
(Śrīmad Bhāgavatam: 9.4.63)[9]

"Although I am free, I still feel as if I am subordinate to My devotees' affection. My devotee surrenders everything and expects nothing in return without My sanction. How can I not give Myself to such surrender? Although constitutionally I am free – still, their attraction, affection, earnestness, sincerity and dependence capture Me. Attracted by My devotees' love, I offer Myself at their behest. They have left everything for Me, how can I cross over them and do anything whimsically, as I like?"

So the clever person who has some idea of devotion, will not take the 'direct' approach – they will go more to the Lord's devotee, than to Him. The Lord is so obliged to His devotees. Kṛṣṇa says, "My devotees can sell Me; they can take Me to the market and sell Me." Mahāprabhu said of Vāsudev Datta, "His devotion to Me is so intense, he can sell Me in the market. Wherever Vāsudev makes a 'market' about Me, I go there to be sold by him – I am so indebted, so closely connected with him."

Śrīla Bhakti Vinod Ṭhākur has sung:

kṛṣṇa se tomāra, kṛṣṇa dite pāra,
tomāra śakati āchhe
āmi ta' kāṅgāla 'kṛṣṇa kṛṣṇa' bali,
dhāi tava pāchhe pāchhe

(O Vaiṣṇava Ṭhākura,) "Kṛṣṇa is yours. You are able to give Him to me, for such is your power. I am indeed wretched and simply run after you, crying 'Kṛṣṇa, Kṛṣṇa!'"[10]

In this way, Bhakti Vinod is looking for the favour of his guru – and his guru in turn, is looking for the favour of his own guru. So, it is a 'telescopic system', and that is the reality. And the peculiarity of this system is, the value of that reality is not diminished, but is enhanced.

So, there is bhakta-saṅga, association of the devotee and Kṛṣṇa-saṅga, the association of Kṛṣṇa. But that Kṛṣṇa-saṅga, is abstract, mostly, so the scripture, śāstra, has given more stress on the association of the devotees: firstly, try to see the Lord there in the devotees, that will be 'concrete' to you. And next, śāstra. So, sādhu-śāstra-kṛpāya, try to get the mercy of the saints and scriptures.

Endnotes to Chapter 12

1 The word Mahāprabhu used for the 'noise' made by the devotees' chanting is kolāhala, which we might render in English as cacophony or even, 'racket' – a disharmonious, disturbing, sound like kitchen pots being clashed together. This shows the Lord's extraordinarily deep samādhi absorption in Kṛṣṇa-līlā, because those who were doing this 'kolāhala' – this chanting of Kṛṣṇa's Name – were not only great, pure, devotees, but also pārṣadas, eternal associates of the Lord, participants directly in Lord Gaurāṅga's līlā. As eternally liberated souls, their vibration of the Holy Name of Kṛṣṇa was certainly pure (Śuddha-Nāma), and yet, Mahāprabhu heard it as 'noise', pulling Him out of the most beautiful experience, and so He expressed His distress and disappointment. It is a lesson. As Śrīla Śrīdhar Mahārāj elsewhere points out, what then can we, aspiring and practising devotees, think about the nature, the purity of our own chanting?

2 The 'telescopic' system is referring to the guru-paramparā: each master in the bona fide lineage is a 'transparent via-medium', like a clear lens, through which the disciple can better 'see' the goal of his search. Just as the more lenses are added in the telescope, the more magnified and clear is the image, so the more gurus through whom the disciple is serving – if they are of course, really pure, like a clear lens, and not 'opaque' – the clearer the image. And because the guru-paramparā is a 'living' system, each guru is contributing also, from their own realisation. It is a spiritual truth – materially speaking, the greater number of 'things' between myself and a distant object, the greater the obstacles – but here, just the opposite.

Although there is some distance, in space and time, between one 'lens' – one guru – and the next, in effect there is none. In Indian philosophy this is known as 'sata-patra-veda-nyāya', the 'logic of a hundred leaves': if you pass a needle through a hundred leaves which are all pressed together, although there is some 'distance' between the leaves, practically the needle passes through them all simultaneously. This is why Śrīla Śrīdhar Mahārāj says the gap between the lenses – the gurus – is 'apparent'.

Another point to note on the subject of 'spiritual magnification' is the fact that unlike material or mundane topics, news, etc., which the more they are discussed become tasteless, hackneyed and old, spiritual talks, on the other hand – talks about the Holy Names, Forms, Qualities, Pastimes and associates of Kṛṣṇa (Hari-kathā) and devotional service – become more and more relishable. They increase, rather than decrease. (That is so for the devotees, and the pious – not the impious or demoniac!) Just as the mango, which is said to become more tasteful when it is 'tasted' by the parrot, so *Śrīmad Bhāgavatam*, which is *nigama-kalpa-taror ghalitaṁ phalaṁ*, the 'ripened fruit of the tree of Vedic knowledge', when it was 'tasted' (heard, received) by Śukadev Goswāmī ('Śuka' also means parrot), it became sweeter, and then in turn when it was delivered by him to Mahārāj Parīkṣit, it became sweeter still. The principle is eternal, and it continues today whenever the *Bhāgavatam* is sung and heard in the association of pure devotees.

3 Śrīla Śrīdhar Mahārāj frequently utilised examples drawn from the material world, to illustrate spiritual points and teachings. He was born in a high-caste family, Bhaṭṭāchārya brāhmaṇas, who are traditionally scholars of the nyāya or logic school, in which the use of analogy is stock-in-trade. Born in 1895, he also had a good English education. In the Calcutta of British India of the early 1900's, the syllabus would include the 'classics' and the work of poets Milton, Coleridge, Shelley, Keats, Shakespeare and others, whom he sometimes quotes. While his analogy here – of going too close to the sun and being burned, being like a person who, though not sufficiently qualified, attempts to have a direct connection with Kṛṣṇa prematurely, without taking shelter of the intermediaries of guru and Vaiṣṇava – is a general example, it reminds us of Icarus, of Greek myth, with which he may have been familiar. (Icarus constructed a pair of wings so he could fly to the sun. Being made of wax, however, they soon melted and Icarus fell to earth.)

4 From *Bhagavad-gītā*, 2.50:

> **buddhi-yukto jahātīha**
> **ubhe sukṛta-duṣkṛte**
> **tasmād yogāya yujyasva**
> **yogaḥ karmasu kauśalam**

"The wise person engaged in devotional service abstains from both good and bad actions in this world; engage yourself therefore in 'yoga', O Arjuna, as yoga is the art of all work."

5 'Big men' – those who are considered important figures in society: lawyers, councillors, mayors, presidents, etc. (In Indian colloquial usage, often called 'big shots'!)

6 Gatekeepers, security guards. (There are also dogs, razor-wire, and nowadays, trip sensors, security lights, CCTV, etc.!)

7 *Samskāra*: acquired psychological tendency; an established conditioned response pattern due to habitual thoughts, words, and actions. This pattern determines the psycho/physical make-up of the embodied jīva-soul which continues from one life, one term of existence, to the next. (The soul itself is actually independent of such conditioning, being spiritual in constitution, but is bound by the samskāras until it gets release from saṁsāra – the 'wheel' of karma, of repeated births and deaths – by the mercy of Kṛṣṇa.)

8 *Yogamāyā*: The particular potency of Kṛṣṇa, who arranges for His Pastimes. She (śaktis or potencies, female) is the potency of 'spiritual illusion'; that is to say, in Kṛṣṇa's abode, she 'covers' the souls there – those who are eternally liberated, and eternal associates of the Lord – so that they do not see, or think, of Kṛṣṇa as 'God', the Supreme Personality of Godhead, but as their master, son, friend or lover. Māyā means illusion ('mā' this, 'yā' not), but this 'illusion' of Yogamāyā is highly desirable for Kṛṣṇa-bhaktas, because it means He can be served in spontaneous love, unencumbered by the awe and

reference with which He is served in Vaikuṇṭha as Lord Nārāyaṇa, or in Ayodhyā as Śrī Rāmachandra, and in other of His Forms.

The 'shadow' aspect of Yogamāyā, who dominates the material creation is Mahāmāyā, the illusory potency which covers all conditioned souls, from Brahmā to the microbe, so that they identify, that is to say misidentify, themselves with matter: "I am this body, and this is mine…"

As Yogamāyā serves Kṛṣṇa in His Pastimes in a particular capacity, Mahāmāyā serves Him by ensuring disobedient souls are purified and reformed by their time in the 'prison' of the material creation, transmigrating from one body to another in different species in the cycle of birth and death, saṁsāra. (Mahāmāyā is also known as Durgā – she from whom it is 'difficult to escape'.) Like a prison governess, she acts fully on behalf of Lord Kṛṣṇa, as His devotee. When souls are fully purified, 'reformed', and dedicated to the service of Lord Kṛṣṇa, then she has no power to keep them incarcerated, and she releases them, to go back home, back to Godhead. As Kṛṣṇa says in *Bhagavad-gītā*, 7.14:

daivī hy eṣā guṇa-mayī
mama māyā duratyayā
mām eva ye prapadyante
māyām etāṁ taranti te

"My alluring 'trimodal' illusory potency is practically insurmountable. However, those who take shelter in Me can overcome this powerful obstacle."

Note: Generally materialistic pious persons, in Indian culture at least, worship Mahāmāyā for material benefits, which she generously gives [she is represented with ten arms!], little realising that increased material comforts are entangling them further into the material 'network of illusion'. Devotees of Kṛṣṇa, rather, worship Rādhārāṇī. Śrī Rādhā is the Ādi-śakti, the original, spiritual potency of Kṛṣṇa, also known as the hlādinī-śakti or pleasure potency, through Whom He is most satisfied.

9 "I am completely under the control of My devotees. Indeed, I am not at all independent. Because My devotees are completely devoid of material desires, I sit only within the cores of their hearts. What to speak of My devotee, even those who are devotees of My devotee are very dear to Me." *(Śrīmad Bhāgavatam: 9.4.63)*

10 A verse of *Śrī Vaiṣṇava-mahimā-gīti* from the compilation *Śaraṇāgati*. The complete bhajan traditionally sung during the vespers or evening prayer in Gauḍīya Vaiṣṇava Temples, is as follows:

(ohe) vaiṣṇava ṭhākura dayāra sāgara
e dāse karuṇā kari
diya pada-chāya śodha he āmāya
tomāra charaṇa dhari

"O worshipable Vaiṣṇava, ocean of grace, be merciful to this servant. Please give me the shade of your feet and purify me. I clasp your feet."

chhaya vega dami' chhaya doṣa śodhi'
chhaya guṇa deha' dāse
chhaya sat-saṅga deha' he āmāre
basechhi saṅgera āśe

"Subjugate the six urges, rectify the six defects, and bestow the six good qualities upon this servitor. Please grant me the six kinds of saintly association, I sit at your feet aspiring for that association."

(Note: The six urges are those of speech, the mind, anger, the tongue, the belly, and the genitals. The six faults are overeating, or collecting more monetary funds than required; over endeavouring for material objectives which are difficult to attain; unnecessary talking about mundane topics; being too attached to, or too neglectful of, Scriptural rules and regulations [due to not knowing or understanding their real aim and purpose]; associating with worldly people; and craving mundane achievements. The six good qualities are enthusiasm, patience, confidence, the determination to perform activities favourable to devotional service, the resolution to abandon the association of non-devotees, and the discipline required to always follow in the footsteps of the previous Āchāryas.)

ekāki āmāra nāhi pāya bala
hari-nāma-saṅkīrtane
tumi kṛpā kari śraddhā-bindu diyā
deha' kṛṣṇa-nāma-dhane

"On my own I have no strength to perform Harināma-saṅkīrtana. Kindly be pleased to bestow a drop of faith in my heart, giving me the treasure of Lord Kṛṣṇa's Name."

kṛṣṇa se tomāra, kṛṣṇa dite pāra,
tomāra śakati āchhe
āmi ta' kāṅgāla 'kṛṣṇa kṛṣṇa' bali,
dhāi tava pāchhe pāchhe

"Kṛṣṇa is yours, you can give Him, you have the power to do so. I who am bereft, calling 'Kṛṣṇa, Kṛṣṇa!' am running desperately behind you. O my Lord, O Vaiṣṇava, ocean of grace, kindly be gracious to this servitor."

Chapter Thirteen

Revealed Truth Unlimited

Intensified Search

Devotee: It seems that sometimes, both in our preaching, and in our devotional service-life in general, though we might be trying our best – with humility, tolerance, and offering respect, as much as we can – there is still so much opposition from people or from the environment. How can we overcome this?

Śrīla Śrīdhar Mahārāj: That opposition will help us to more intensively search for a higher plane. The decision, the absolute decision about what comes to us, that comes from the upper level, and it will help us to search for the higher plane more intensely. We will have to examine ourselves, whether the path I have taken, is it only imagination, or is any reality there? "Kṛṣṇa is everything, and He protects His devotees" – such statement, is it only theoretical, or is it real? We must make experiments with this truth in our own life, and we will make progress, step by step.

Such tests will be extended to us by Kṛṣṇa Himself: "Do you have faith in Me as Absolute, or in any other party, that they are your master?"

Is your faith only 'lip-deep'? When you say that "Kṛṣṇa is everything, He is over all" – is it a lip-deep statement, or does it really come from your heart, and conscience? To say, "Nothing can be done without His consent, nothing may happen without His will" – is this all imaginary propaganda, or is it real? Is it a reality to live in, and live on, or only something to 'preach'?

Real Life Within

To be always eager for the fight, that is not a very high stage.[1] But, to ignore the fight: "My environment, that which surrounds me, let it go on in its own way, and I shall be busy with my own things, my own duties. The opposing elements, they will come as a consequence of my previous life's actions.[2] Let them come, but to my back, not in my front." We shall show our back to them, and many wounds may come there; but in the front, there will be peace, and Kṛṣṇa. We will progress towards that side, towards Him. We will think: "The results of my previous activities, they have come to get their satisfaction and they may attack me, but that will be from behind. Ignoring them, I shall make progress forwards, towards my Lord."

So, Kṛṣṇa is everything – but that must be realised as truth within me, otherwise what value does such a statement have? It would be only lip-deep propaganda. There must be life within us, to back the preaching. The words that come from our mouth must be backed by spiritual realisation, that "Kṛṣṇa *is* all in all."

A Manipur Incident

There is a history which occurred here in India over 100 years ago during the time of British rule in Manipur. At that time all the residents of Manipur state, including the King, were Vaiṣṇavites, disciples descending from Narottama Ṭhākur.

One Indian Army General, his name was General Tikendrajit, wanted to overthrow the influence of the British in Manipur, and he was using as his military depot the compound of the Rādhā-Govinda Temple there. The British received some intelligence about this, and a military officer was sent to investigate, but the Rāj, the King of Manipur, did not allow that man, a European and a 'mlechchha',[3] to enter into the Temple compound. However, he forcibly entered, and General Tikendrajit had him murdered, killed, at once. Then a British force was sent to capture the depot, with special instructions that the Temple compound, which had been used for political and military purposes, must be demolished. The force of the bombardment by cannon-shot was so heavy that the whole temple was destroyed and the Deities, also, were demolished.

Unlimited Kṛṣṇa

Our Guru Mahārāj, Śrīla Bhakti Siddhānta Saraswatī Ṭhākur, related this story to us, and explained the meaning. Because in such an incident, the general perception may be: "What is this? The Deities, Who have been worshipped for generations by the disciples of Narottama Ṭhākur, did not have the power to protect Themselves? Kṛṣṇa had no power to protect Himself? Then, the Deities are all idols, dolls."

But Prabhupāda explained it in another way. He asked, "Without the will of Kṛṣṇa, nothing can happen, so, was it the will of Kṛṣṇa that His worshipable Figure should be destroyed by the shot of a cannon? If nothing can occur, even a straw cannot move, without the will of Kṛṣṇa, then if such a great disaster was done, was that also by His will? Yes? Then, why?"

First he quoted this śloka:

archye viṣṇau śilā-dhīr guruṣu
nara-matir vaiṣṇave jāti-buddhir
viṣṇor vā vaiṣṇavānāṁ kali-mala-
mathane pāda-tīrthe 'mbu-buddhiḥ
śrī-viṣṇor nāmni mantre sakala-kaluṣa-he
śabda-sāmānya-buddhir
viṣṇau sarveśvareśe tad-itara-sama-dhīr
yasya vā nārakī saḥ
(Padma Purāṇa)

"Whoever considers the Deity of the Supreme Lord to be dead matter made out of wood, stone or metal; or the spiritual master, who is an eternal servant of the Supreme Lord, to be an ordinary man, who is prone to die; or the Vaiṣṇava to be coming from some caste; or the water that washes the feet of the pure devotee or the Supreme Personality of Godhead to be ordinary water, although such water has the potency to destroy all the evils of the Age of Kali; or who considers the Holy Name of the Supreme Lord or mantras dedicated to Him, which are able to destroy all sin, to be ordinary sounds; or thinks the Supreme Lord of all, Lord Viṣṇu, to be on the same level as demigods, has a hellish mentality. Whoever thinks in this way is certainly a resident of hell."

We generally identify as spiritual truth that which comes down in this world to help us, in a particular form, such as the Deity. That is given in the scriptures, and we are encouraged to see in that way, but, as our Guru Mahārāj explained, at the same time, that is not the same as the wholesale Spiritual Reality. So, to do away with our wrong conception – that what we see, the Deity, that "It is Kṛṣṇa" – to demolish that wrong idea, this was done (the destruction of the Deity) by Kṛṣṇa's own will. Is it clear?

Devotee: Yes, Mahārāj.

The Lord as Śrī Vigraha

Śrīla Śrīdhar Mahārāj: In the Deity, the Lord and the connection of the conscious spiritual plane have come to this mundane plane of our sense experience, so, the Deity should not be neglected or reckoned as an idol. Outwardly, if we exercise our physical senses, the Śrī Mūrti may be of stone, or wood, or any mineral substance, but we are not to look at that. We should try to see that the Lord is attracted here by the affection and love of the sādhus. As with the purifying capacity in Ganges water, so the purifying presence of the Śrī Vigraha is independent of our physical senses and calculative mind. It transcends all the stages of knowledge which can be collected from sense experience. At the same time, however, the Deity conception, the presence of the Lord in this form, is considered to be 'primary', the lowest; the Deity is a presence of the Lord, but in a 'gross' way. Above that is the śāstra, the scripture. And when we can trace the existence of the Lord in the heart of the devotees, our position becomes higher, we moved to a nearer realisation of Godhead.

Vaiṣṇava, Śāstra, Vigraha, Tīrtha

In the Vaiṣṇava, the truth is animated more than in the Vigraha (the Deity), the Tīrtha (holy place of pilgrimage)[4], or the śāstra (scripture). We find a direct connection with Kṛṣṇa in the consciousness of a Vaiṣṇava. Faith in the devotees, the Vaiṣṇavas, grants us the most substantial help. The devotees are above even the śāstra, the scriptures.

There are some who want to know about Kṛṣṇa only from the śāstra. In the almanac it is written that this year so much rain is expected, so much rain will come. But if we press the almanac, will a drop of water ooze out of it? The śāstra is something like that – it says 'do this', 'do that', but the śāstra cannot give us Kṛṣṇa. First we get the direction from śāstra, then we are to do as it advises, we are to practise.[5] But, still, we are mainly helpless when searching with this method, or that method.

Practically, we should come in connection with the service of a Vaiṣṇava. I am to serve, but I can't come directly in connection with Him, with the Lord – so, who can I serve? The Deity Form of the Lord, the Vigraha, is there, the śāstra is there – but in a sense these are superficial. The real substance we find in a Vaiṣṇava, in his heart. *Dharmasya tattvaṁ nihitaṁ guhāyāṁ.*[6] The Kṛṣṇa conception, Kṛṣṇa as He is, all knowledge and love, we find living in the heart of a Vaiṣṇava who directs all his activities towards His service.

Misconception Demolished

So, the verse, *archye Viṣṇau śilā-dhīr...*, says that by knowing things only superficially, we are really pilgrims to hell. What we see, Kṛṣṇa in the form of 'stone' – the Deity – Kṛṣṇa is there, no doubt, but He is not limited there, limited to such a form. So our Guru Mahārāj explained that to do away with such a conception, Kṛṣṇa takes such a bold step, allowing His Deity to be 'broken', to show that "I am not your sense-conceived, eye-conceived 'stone-form', I am something else."

It is to elevate you to a higher understanding from the lowest position of understanding the nature of the Deity, that is, the presence of Divinity as the Deity – to demolish that limited conception in you and give you a higher type of understanding.

It is something like the 'national flag'. The flag represents the honour of the nation, but supposing in war the flag is captured by the enemy and trodden under foot. Of course, when the flag is dishonoured, it means the nation's honour is demolished, but still we have to think that the nation remains. It exists, though its honour, its freedom and its independence, which is represented by the flag, is destroyed. Even when the flag is torn to pieces, or trampled under foot, burned to ashes, or otherwise destroyed, the nation's integrity and independence is there, and again that nation may come back and conquer their foe. In this way, though the flag represents the country and its freedom, it does not represent the whole of its freedom. The nation's freedom, its independent existence, is not 'contained', is not limited there.

So, the Vigraha, the Deity Form of the Lord, is necessary. It is a symbol given to us, and we are encouraged to see that it is the Lord, it is He, Himself, and not otherwise; but still, we must try to go further in our conception, that He is not what we can conceive with our senses. He is not limited to that. We have to differentiate there.

Progress always means elimination and new acceptance. Śrīla Bhakti Vinod Ṭhākur says that we should always be free, unprejudiced, to accept truth; we should always be expectant, by comparative study, to understand revealed truth in deeper ways.[7]

Endnotes to Chapter 13

1 The 'fight' with the environment – be it people, circumstances, events, etc. This material world is known as Devī-dhām, the world of the Devī, that is, controlled by Prakṛti-devī or Durgā, the mistress of illusory energy. She is working, in turn, under the control of the

Supreme Lord, Kṛṣṇa, and as such is His representative and devotee. In a sense, for a conditioned soul to take up the study and practice of devotional service, Kṛṣṇa consciousness is, as the Āchāryas have said – and the experience of practising devotees confirms it – to "declare war against māyā, the illusory energy"; also, that "preaching means a fight." This is so, indeed, for the madhyama-adhikārī, or devotee in the 'middle stage' of Kṛṣṇa-realisation.

Here, however, Śrīla Śrīdhar Mahārāj shows us another level, ultimately a higher level, of 'adjustment with the environment'. As he says, "the opposing elements will come as a result of my previous actions – let them come, I will go on with my service." He would often also say, "Don't blame the environment." And he had a nicely nuanced version of the English proverb "a bad workman quarrels with his tools" – that is, "a bad workman quarrels with his stools!" Stool comes as a result of what one has eaten – what is the point of quarrelling with it? That is only a waste of energy. The positive course is to change one's eating habits!

2 'Previous life's actions' – actions previously performed in this present life, or indeed, karmic results of actions performed in one's previous life or lives.

3 *Mlechchha*: refers to non-Āryan peoples, here referring not to a particular human race, as such, but to those who do not observe behaviours according to Vedic, or similarly developed socio-spiritual, principles – more specifically, those accustomed to cow-killing, which from a Vedic view is considered barbarian, uncivilised.

4 Religious biographer Shirley du Boulay writes: "A desire to stand on holy ground, to be in a place where the veil between heaven and earth has grown thin, seems to be a deep human instinct."
(*A Silent Melody,* p.91)

It might seem paradoxical that though God is indeed everywhere, one should seek Him in special places. Śrīla Śrīdhar Mahārāj gives the analogy that the King is present everywhere throughout the land, through his 'energy' – his representatives, his institutions, etc. – but he is personally present in a special way, in his own palace. For Vaiṣṇavas, the tīrtha, or holy place of pilgrimage, is a manifestation of the Lord, and as such is considered non-different from Him. There are many such tīrthas in India, places where the Lord or His Incarnations appeared, or manifested Their eternal Pastimes (līlā) on this earth. (A meaning of 'tīrtha' is 'fording-place' – like a ford in a river, a place where one can easily and safely cross over to the other side – a tīrtha is a place where the 'veil between the worlds' is thin.) The word 'dhāma' also means a holy place; although this usually refers to a larger area – Vṛndāvan-dhāma or Purī-dhāma, for example – a tract of land, rather than a particular shrine, or temple, etc. When such holy places are approached with humility and respect, they can be a source of great blessings for the pilgrim.

Many, of course, visit tīrthas and dhāmas to pray for blessings for ordinary or mundane purposes – wealth, health, good marriage, education, etc. They may indeed get such a result, also, but as Lord Kṛṣṇa says in *Bhagavad-gītā* (7.23), these fruits are temporary:

antavat tu phalaṁ teṣāṁ
tad bhavaty alpa-medhasām
devān deva-yajo yānti
mad-bhaktā yānti mām api

"But the fruit obtained by those unwise worshippers of the demigods is temporary. They reach the gods they worship, but My devotees come to Me."

They are like a person who approaches one of the King's ministers and requests a handful of coins, whereas the King himself can give immense wealth. In any case, the potency of the 'ministers' (demigods) itself is delegated from the King. (Kṛṣṇa further says that demigod-worship is really meant for Him but is offered without proper understanding. It is He, Who gives the results through the agency of the demigods.) The Vedic scriptures say also, that one who goes to the 'dhāma' only to take bath in the holy rivers there, but does not visit, honour, or enquire from the holy persons (sādhus) living there, is no better than a donkey!

It is said the holy dhāma in its reality is hidden to material vision under the covering of māyā, Kṛṣṇa's illusory potency. So devotees pray to the Lord to remove this covering so they can see the 'dhāma'. In this present age (kali-yuga) Nabadwīp Dhāma (in Bengal, India) is said to be the best of all holy places, because the very incarnation of mercy, Śrī Chaitanya Mahāprabhu, appeared there.

[5] Śrīla Śrīdhar Mahārāj is here looking at śāstra and sādhu, scriptures and saints, comparatively and, as such, is explaining that the śāstra is giving a more passive kind of guidance, and the sādhu, more active, thus establishing that for the spiritual practitioner, the association of sādhu is immediately of greater importance. Śrī Chaitanya Mahāprabhu said that of the 64 items in devotional service, the absolutely most important are sādhu-saṅga, holy association, and Kṛṣṇa-nāma, chanting of the Lord's Holy Name. Of course, as a whole, all elements work together in devotional service, as is said: *guru, śāstra, sādhu-vākya chittete koriyā aikya* – with the help of guru, scripture and sādhu, and then confirmation from within the heart from the inner-guru (chaitya-guru) one is to progress. And one's ability, or capacity, in being able to clearly discern and to follow these directions depends on the maturity of one's śraddhā, faith.

This having been said, in one sense śāstra, scripture, is pre-eminent. As one Āchārya has put it: "books are the basis." Indeed, Śrīla Śrīdhar Mahārāj himself was renowned for his deep love for, and understanding of, the scriptures; he was awarded the title 'Śāstra-nipuṇa' by his guru, for his abilities in this regard. Traditionally, in any spiritual discussion between paṇḍits (scholars) in India, any point put forward would have to be supported by scriptural quotation, chapter and verse – or it would not even be taken seriously.

The holy Veda, Vedic-knowledge, is considered a non-different manifestation from the Lord – God in sound-form. In *Bhagavad-Gītā*, Kṛṣṇa says:

vedaiś cha sarvair aham eva vedyo
vedānta-kṛd veda-vid eva chāham
(Śrīmad Bhagavad-gītā: 15:15)

"I alone am the Sweet Absolute to be known through all the Vedas. I am the revealer of the *Vedānta* – Vedavyāsa – and I am the knower of the Vedas."

(*Vedānta* is the concise form of Vedic knowledge, therefore also known as the *Vedānta-sūtras*. The sage Vedavyāsa, compiler of the Vedas, is himself an empowered incarnation of the Lord, Nārāyaṇa, Kṛṣṇa's plenary expansion, and is sometimes referred to as the literary incarnation of God.)

The principle of śabda-brahma, divine sound, being non-different from that which it represents – unlike sound in the world of duality, which is different therefrom – is a subject beyond the scope of these comments. But, the Vedic principle that the very creation of the material cosmos itself, proceeds from sound vibration, is echoed in many theist traditions – Judaism, Islam, Christianity.

Saint John's Gospel begins: "In the beginning was the Word, and the Word was with God, and the Word was God… the same was in the beginning, with God. All things were made by Him, and without Him was not made anything that was made…" *(King James V, John, 1–3)*

Theistic traditions all hold, also, that God has created human beings unique among all creatures, with a prevenient receptivity to divine revelation. As Jesuit theologian Karl Rahner put it: as humans, we are specifically 'hearers of the Word'. Revelation can also come through the 'book of nature', or through inner experience, it is true, and these are available to all men – but careful attention to scripture, when prayerfully imbibed into a purified heart, can give revelation which is super-rational, or transcendental.

Michael Casey OCSO (Order of Cistercians of the Strict Observance) writes:

"The historic word of revelation is not a 'thing', it is a force, a power, a dynamism. 'The word of God is living and active, sharper than every two-edged sword. It penetrates even to the division of soul and spirit, joints and marrow; and it judges the thoughts and dispositions of the heart.' (*Heb.* 4:12). The Word is not merely an external 'word' that provides us with information. God's word is a power for salvation that links up with something within us and draws forth from our depths a latent desire to make contact with God." (From *Grace, on the Journey to God* p.140).

But in order for this effect to take place, one has to 'receive the Word' in humility. In the *New Testament*, Saint James writes in his Epistle: "Receive with meekness the implanted Word, for it has power to save your souls." (*Jas.* 1:21). In Vaiṣṇava language, this is referred to as 'submissive aural reception'. It happens in two ways: by hearing from people of faith, especially those who are advanced, developed on the spiritual path, and with whom one feels a level of 'harmonious resonance' (one is not going to be 'submissive', or submission will only be forced, in the association of someone in whose presence one feels less than comfortable!); also through private, spiritual reading. This is called, in Christian theology, 'lectio divina' (divine reading) – a slow, prayerful and meditative reading of scripture, in order to enter into what is being said, to internalise it. This 'lectio divina' is the precursor to meditation and prayer; it will naturally lead to them.

A common reason why spiritual practitioners of any faith-tradition find themselves 'blocked' in prayer is that they have become lax, or greatly diminished, in their spiritual reading. In the words of *Psalm* 102 (v.5), "they forgot to eat their bread" (as in the 'Lord's prayer', "Give us this day our daily bread"). Evelyn Underhill, who wrote much on the subject of prayer in its different stages, said: "Spiritual reading is, or at least can be, second only to prayer as a developer and supporter of the inner life"; and in *The Message of the Wesleys*, a book on spirituality of the

Methodist school: "it cannot be that people should grow in grace unless they give themselves to reading." So this is a very important component in spiritual life. (This is the general principle. Specifically, of course, there may be, both in Vaiṣṇavism or in other traditions, those saints and savants who, while being even uneducated or illiterate, are, or have become in their lifetime, by special grace, fully God-realised, without 'reading' at all; the Lord reveals His truth to them, from within their heart.)

It should also be mentioned that there are different levels of meaning to be distinguished in the scriptures. This has been elucidated in the Vaiṣṇava tradition by eminent scholars such as Śrī Jīva Goswāmī, who in his scriptural exegesis distinguishes literal, subjective, and esoteric meanings in the Vedic texts. In Christianity, since the time of Origen of Alexandria in the 3rd century, different levels of meaning in the Bible, Old Testament and New, have also been distinguished. The obvious meaning of the scriptural text, Origen named the 'literal' or 'historical' sense – this is accessible to a general or casual reader, and can be further investigated for its 'authenticity', 'historicity', etc, by even non-believing scholars. Beyond this, however is a world of meaning that becomes apparent only under the radiance of faith, it then naturally stirs up the desire for prayer within us, and lifts up the heart to the Lord. If one reads scripture only as a narrative, or a source of information, historical or otherwise, valuable as this may be, one will miss totally the profound and existential meaning that the text is meant to produce in the heart of the faithful.

6 *Dharmasya tattvaṁ nihitaṁ guhāyāṁ.* This line occurs in a verse from *Mahābhārata* (*Vana-parva*, 313.117). The verse says, essentially: "The real truth, dharma (that which in the most essential way, or that which holds or supports the soul) is hidden in the heart of the great souls, the devotees." Thus Śrīla Śrīdhar Mahārāj says here, "The real substance we find in a Vaiṣṇava, in his heart."

This verse was spoken by the Pāṇḍava Yudhiṣṭhir in answer to the question, "What is dharma?" (That is, "Where is the Truth?")

This was put to him by Yamarāj, god of death, who had taken the form of a lake bird to test him. (It was one of a hundred essential questions – "What is the News?" "What is the most Astonishing?" "Who is Happy?" … – to all of which Yudhiṣṭhir gave penetrating and wonderful answers, and thus highly satisfied Yamarāj.)

Mahārāj Yudhiṣṭhir said:

tarko 'pratiṣṭhaḥ śrutayo vibhinnā
nāsāv ṛṣir yasya mataṁ na bhinnam
dharmasya tattvaṁ nihitaṁ guhāyāṁ
mahājano yena gataḥ sa panthāḥ

Śrīla B.S. Govinda Mahārāj concisely translates: "Reasoning is inconclusive. The scriptures are of many varieties. One whose conception is not distinctive cannot become a ṛṣi (spiritual professor). True dharma is thus secretly concealed. Therefore, the way of the Mahājans, great souls, is the path."

Answering first in the negative, Yudhiṣṭhir said to the bird (Yamarāj) *tarko 'pratiṣṭhaḥ*: "Sir, the truth cannot be ascertained, and cannot be understood, by argument." Argument may go on for endless time, and that based also not on speculation but on the Vedas themselves, and the various commentaries and opinions of the sages based thereon. The sages of different qualities, backgrounds and schools of thought will all see from their own perspectives and will give their evidence as 'filtered' accordingly, and that must be partial, at best. But the truth is nirguṇa, devoid of mundane or material qualities, it is not subject to any such treatment or process and cannot be 'captured' thereby; no amount of arguments can bring it out. It is a secret thing, a hidden treasure, it is independent of the intellectual attempt. How can intellect capture spirit? It is not possible: *dharmasya tattvaṁ nihitaṁ guhāyāṁ*. How, then?

Yudhiṣṭhir Mahārāj said that you can find that Hidden Treasure, the Truth, only in the heart of the devotee of the Lord (Mahājan). Why? Because the Lord Himself is living there. He is living Truth. Śrī Kṛṣṇa told Nārada Ṛṣi in *Śrīmad Bhāgavatam*, "I am not where the yogīs are meditating, where the charity givers are giving… I am where My devotee is loving Me, he is always praising and singing about Me, worshipping Me, adoring Me heart and soul." Kṛṣṇa reveals Himself to His pure devotee. He says in *Bhagavad-gītā* to Arjuna, that He is revealing knowledge of Himself to him because "You are My very dear friend." (See 10.1, 18.64, 18.65). He openly declares that He has no independence from the will of His devotee, as in the case of Ambarīṣa Mahārāj and Durvāsā Muni (*aham bhakta-parādhīnaḥ*, SB: 9.4.63). In fact He enjoys Himself playing within His devotees' hearts ('*tomāra hṛdaye sadā Govinda-viśrām Govinda kahena – mora Vaiṣṇava-parāṇa*' from *Prārthanā* by Śrīla Bhakti Vinod Ṭhākur).

Śrīla B.S. Govinda Mahārāj comments: "Yudhiṣṭhir Mahārāj said, 'We cannot take the advice of the Vedas directly. Our store of knowledge is very limited, and the knowledge given in the Vedas is very vast. The Vedas explain pratyakṣa-jñāna (sensory knowledge), parokṣa-jñāna (collective knowledge), aparokṣa-jñāna (subtle knowledge), and adhokṣaja-jñāna (transcendental knowledge). Also, the many ṛṣis who describe Vedic knowledge, present many different interpretations of it, and are not always perfect… Thus the jīva-souls become confused; they cannot find the truth with only the scriptures, the differing opinions of the ṛṣis, and their own minds. To find the proper conception we must follow the path of the Mahājans, the great souls, in whose hearts the truth is living.'" (*Revealed Truth,* p.40)

Note: 'Mahājan', or great soul, great personage, here refers specifically to Vaiṣṇavas, devotees of the Lord. Although all great devotees can be considered Mahājans, in *Śrīmad Bhāgavatam* (6.3.20), Vyāsadev indicated twelve 'Mahājans' specifically: Lord Brahmā, Nārada Ṛṣi, Lord Śiva, the four Kumāras, Kapiladev, Manu, Prahlāda Mahārāj, Janaka Rāj, Bhīṣmadev, Bali Mahārāj, Śukadev Goswāmī, and Yamarāj. These twelve, and their teachings on devotional service, are described throughout the scriptures. Their primary qualification is that they are devotees of the Lord. While the 'Mahājans' give the primary and essential teachings of the Vedic devotional lineage – similar somewhat to the role of the nine principal gurus of the Sikhs, or the thirty-three 'Doctors' of the Roman Catholic Church, in their own traditions – for the practising devotee, it is very helpful to have śikṣa, spiritual advice and guidance, and example, 'closer to home', that is, as embodied in a living teacher. This brings us back again, to the prime importance of sādhu, the saint, in relation to the more 'passive' advice of the śāstra, the scripture.

In his book *A Path through the Desert*, Benedictine Father Anselm Grun has selected and commented on forty of the 1,000 or so 'apophthegmata patrum' or 'sayings of the Fathers', the hermits who populated the deserts of Sinai and Egypt in the third to sixth centuries. These sayings have been carefully preserved in the Eastern Orthodox tradition. Here we find, for example:

"Someone asked Abba Paesius 'What should I do about my soul, because it is insensitive and does not fear God?'

"He said to him, 'Go and join a man who fears God, and live near him; he will teach you too, to fear God.'" (Poemen 65)

Fr. Grun writes: "An encounter with a mature person often provides the best form of schooling. This applies also to the spiritual life. The young monk who comes to see Abba Paesius has certainly heard much about God. He has had a religious education. But the words about God do not penetrate into his heart. His heart remains unmoved. He does not allow himself to be touched by God. It would make no sense for him to read more or reflect more on God. Everything would remain in the head. It is not much use learning spiritual techniques. The will alone cannot open the heart to God and induce it to fear Him or feel His presence. When we 'go to school' with someone who fears God, who allows themselves to be touched by God in their heart, then our heart, too, will slowly open up. But it will not be enough to just listen to the words of this person. We should also observe them closely to examine whether they live what they say… When we recognise that everything the other person does is in harmony, then something in ourselves, too, will be transformed. Then the longing within us is stirred, the longing to be touched by God, for our heart to be broken open. The closeness to a person who is penetrated by God, in turn leads us to God… (in them) we get a glimpse of the light and the love of God, which shines in them." (*A Path through the Desert,* pp.53–4)

Note: The Biblical expression, to 'fear God', as used in the above, does not of course mean to be 'afraid' of God, as such, but to have a clear awareness of His might and majesty, as in the biblical statement, "Fear of the Lord is the beginning of wisdom." Also, as a caveat to the above quotation, Vaiṣṇava teachings warn us not to 'judge' the devotee by his or her external symptoms, or not by these alone. They are one kind of indicator, but the 'substance' of the devotee is not always reflected in the manner of their 'form'. And, related to this, close personal proximity to a pure devotee on the part of a neophyte practitioner may, indeed, not always be helpful for them. Since 'familiarity breeds contempt', through mundane vision they may see only the apparent, material aspects of the devotee, so, believing them to be not 'spiritual' but material and contemptible, will make offences, even if only mentally. This results – since such behaviour in relation to His pure devotee is not pleasing to the Lord – in denser coverings by material illusion over that person's soul, and, in turn, their own distancing from devotional service.

[7] The four items discussed in this chapter – the devotee, the scripture, the Vigraha or Deity, and the holy place – are all understood as manifestations of the Lord. Of pre-eminent importance in the life of a devotee, also, is 'Nāma' – the Holy Name of the Lord, which is a non-different manifestation of the Lord Himself. Along with sādhu-saṅga, association with pure devotees, the chanting of the Holy Name is the most important item of devotional service. Though the truth of the Holy Name (Nāma-tattva) is not specifically discussed in this chapter, this most important subject has been elaborately and beautifully elucidated upon by Śrīla Śrīdhar Mahārāj elsewhere in many of his talks and writings. (See especially, for example, in the book *Search for Śrī Kṛṣṇa, Reality the Beautiful* pp.133–173).

Part III

The Way of Surrender

from informal discourses
by
Śrīla Bhakti Rakṣak Śrīdhar
Dev-Goswāmī Mahārāj

With contemporary endnote explanations by
Śrī Bhakti Swarūp Tridaṇḍi Mahārāj

Chapter Fourteen

Association of the Holy

The Different Forms of Devotion

Śrīla Śrīdhar Mahārāj: We need association of the holy, with our surrender. According to the intensity of surrender, one may have the association of the higher devotee, and that will help one to make progress fairly, properly, and quickly.
Devotee: Surrender is known as ātma-nivedana?
Śrīla Śrīdhar Mahārāj: Yes. And after ātma-nivedana, then śravaṇa, kīrtana, smaraṇa, vandana… (hearing, chanting, remembering, praying…). There are different forms of devotion, but all are in ātma-nivedana – their basis is ātma-nivedana, self-surrender.
Devotee: Generally, we hear that ātma-nivedana is given as the last in the nine kinds of devotion, after śravaṇa, kīrtana…
Śrīla Śrīdhar Mahārāj: The last? It is in the beginning, also; it is everything, and everywhere! (Laughter.) Without ātma-nivedana, self-surrender, no śravaṇa, hearing, is possible; and, vice-versa, without hearing surrender won't increase. They are interdependent, and it is so with all the limbs of devotion. They are all one, they are all bhakti. Without surrender, none of the devotional practices can be bhakti; but, without hearing, and other practices which are based on a soul's sukṛti, spiritual fortune, ātma-nivedana, surrender may not come. So, although for the purpose of our understanding, they are represented to us in different ways, or in a certain order – hearing, then chanting,

then remembering, and so on – they are all interdependent, and helping each other, and in this sense are one and the same. One part presupposes another. Śravaṇa, hearing, comes first – but, without kīrtana, without chanting, how can there be hearing? How can you hear, if there is no chanting?[1] And then smaraṇa, remembering – without such mental recollection, such memory, how can there be hearing, and chanting? All are interdependent.

Devotee: So, surrender is one's attitude, and service is the activity?

Śrīla Śrīdhar Mahārāj: No, not 'attitude'. Surrender is not attitude, it is the innate nature of the soul, but it is covered at present by different kinds of 'dirt'. The innate wealth, the innermost wealth of every jīva, every soul, is surrender. And service means surrender, it exists on the basis of surrender. "I serve." "I dedicate." Dedication, service, surrender – they all are similar.

All-Loving Environment

The nature, the very conception of the Vaikuṇṭha world is service, and there every soul is unlimitedly surrendered, living only for the good of others. It is just the opposite here in the material world, where every unit wants to exploit another. Exploitation is in the plane of māyā, misconception. It exists only on the 'cover', the covering of the soul, but the innate substance of the soul is surrender, self-surrender. So, in the Vaikuṇṭha world all are 'mad' to help their neighbour, to look after the interest of others in connection with the Supreme Power. That is the innate wealth, the innate nature, of every unit, of everything there. All-cooperation. All-goodness. All-cooperation at the cost of one's own life. It is the nature of the inhabitants of Vaikuṇṭha and Goloka. How happy it is!

But such degree of self-sacrificing requires that one must, in Hegel's expression, 'Die to live'[2]. This means, to dissolve your ego, your false ego, wholesale and then you will find your causal self, your true self. The sham, false, ego, that must be dissolved, then all doubts will be eliminated, and you will find that you are quite at home.[3]

Surrender and Serve

Devotee: You have said that service and surrender are like the two rails of a track.

Śrīla Śrīdhar Mahārāj: Yes. They are like the two wheels on which bhakti is running. There is surrender, and on the basis of surrender, there is service, and that is movement, progress, towards the object of one's surrender. Without surrender no bhakti can come, and the nature of one's surrender will be traced in service. The two, surrender and service, are co-existent. It is like the plan, and the work. There is a design, and work according to the design. Surrender is there, and on that basis activity, service, is going on. Both must be present. So, surrender is not only a static thing, not merely a 'plane of being', but it is dynamic. Everything in creation, in existence, is dynamic, is progressive, and surrender is also dynamic. It has life, it increases.[4]

Beyond Estimation

Surrender is also of different types: the surrender of a friend, surrender of a wife, surrender of the parents, and so on. It may be of many different kinds.

Devotee: What is the highest kind of service, of surrender?

Śrīla Śrīdhar Mahārāj: That is found in consorthood. Twenty-four hours per day service is possible there. Love in consorthood has been shown to bc of thc highest type, both in surrender, and in service. Surrender to the extreme, and service to the extreme, that is found only in consorthood. And within that, also there are different types, and Rādhārāṇī is considered to be the highest. This means that everything – the full serving-potency – is coming out from Her. She is the main 'predominated moiety', the predominated aspect of Divinity. The entire 'negative side', the serving aspect, is represented by Her, and others are all different developments from Her. Her position is such. It cannot be estimated in our 'puppy brain'! (Laughter). It is beyond our estimation.

Kṛṣṇa-Confidence

Mahāprabhu, Śrī Chaitanyadev, Who is Rādhā and Kṛṣṇa combined, came to inform us about this, and to tell us that by getting our admission in this line – serving under the divine guidance of Rādhārāṇī – we may have experience of such highest quality of rasa, such taste of divine love. That line is called the Rūpānuga-sampradāya, and it is the speciality of Mahāprabhu and His followers.

This may seem like mere stories, like tales, to us at present. But nevertheless, such a prospect has been given to us. If we are able to find it out, gradually, such is our goal, our destination. It is such a high conception, such 'Kṛṣṇa-confidence', that we can get the confidence of Kṛṣṇa, get admission into the confidential service of Kṛṣṇa, and of such a high type, and that our future may be connected with that!

"I Am Yours"

Devotee: I read in a book that śaraṇāgati is only a mental attitude, whereas ātma-nivedana is full surrender of the soul.

Śrīla Śrīdhar Mahārāj: (Laughs.) No, no. Whoever says that śaraṇāgati is mental, is on the mental level, they are wrong. Mind cannot even touch that level, that plane of śaraṇāgati. Mind is produced from the workshop of māyā.

Devotee: Then, śaraṇāgati and ātma-nivedana are the same?

Śrīla Śrīdhar Mahārāj: When śaraṇāgati is analysed, then we find six elements there:

ānukūlyasya saṅkalpaḥ
prātikūlyasya varjanam
rakṣiṣyatīti viśvāso
goptṛtve varaṇaṁ tathā
ātma-nikṣepa-kārpaṇye
ṣaḍ-vidhā śaraṇāgatiḥ

(Hari-bhakti-vilāsa: 11.676, quoted in
Śrī Chaitanya-charitāmṛta, Madhya-līlā: 22.100)

"The six divisions of surrender are: to accept those things favourable for devotional service, to reject unfavourable things, the conviction that Kṛṣṇa will give all protection, to accept the Lord as one's guardian or master, full self-surrender, and humility."

Within these six parts of śaraṇāgati, Jīva Goswāmī Prabhu points out that goptṛtve varaṇaṁ, to accept the Lord as Master, as Guardian, that "I am Yours", this embracing of the Lord's guardianship, is the central element and the others are all supportive to it. So, in śaraṇāgati, as it is described in the śāstra, we find that ātma-nivedana, 'full self-surrender', constitutes its one part, and another part is ātma-nikṣepa, to 'throw oneself, desperately' to the Lord. But they are not, in themselves, the essential part of śaraṇāgati. Most principal, most central, is goptṛtvc varaṇam: to accept Him, the Lord, as one's Master and Guardian. That, "I am Yours" – this is the most vital, central point of śaraṇāgati, and not, to 'throw oneself'. One may throw oneself anywhere and everywhere, but there must be some Guardian, and the sense that, "I am at His disposal." That is the central thought of śaraṇāgati.

Where to 'Throw Yourself'?

Of course, in a more spacious way, when we look at śaraṇāgati, we see that it embodies, it includes so many parts – to do what is favourable for surrender and service to the Lord, to avoid what is unfavourable to that, and so on, – but the main thing, the central nature of śaraṇāgati is this: "I am Yours."

Merely throwing oneself desperately to any place, that also is not safe! Such desperate bravery we can see is shown by different people for different purposes – for political ends, for national freedom – there are so many examples of great risk in self-sacrifice. But that in itself won't come under the jurisdiction of śaraṇāgati.

Sacrifice as ātma-nivedana, full surrender of one's self, means it must be located in the proper place, that is, to have the Guardian. We must know we have a Guardian, and that we belong to Him, and that we shall give back to Him what is His – that is, our self. "I am Yours. For so long I was thinking that 'I belong to me'. Now I have come to understand that I don't belong to me. You are my owner and I am Your slave. I am Your dependent, a part of Your potency. I am not independent. I am Yours – neither do I belong to me, nor to any other, to so many so-called 'friends' or 'foes' in the world, nor to anything else such as the earth, or the sun, or air, or ether, or anything. I belong to You, Kṛṣṇa.

"I belong only to You. And, what are You? You are 'Kṛṣṇa' the Attracting Centre of everything that exists."

Drawn to Love's Centre

Kṛṣṇa is the All-attracting Principle. Attraction – in the plane of consciousness, that becomes affection, love. Attraction is there in the physical plane, such as the sun attracting the earth, the earth attracting so many things. This is physical, but when it is endowed with life, when it is spirit, spirit-filled, that is prema, love, and that love is in relation to the Highest Entity, the All-Attractor, the Personification of Love. Through prema we belong to Him. And by love's influence there is mercy, harmony, beauty, and they are all divine, and they are all subservient to love. The highest conception of Divinity is love.

Endnotes to Chapter 14

[1] Śrīla Śrīdhar Mahārāj is explaining that all the 'forms' of devotion (hearing about the Lord, chanting His Names and Glories, remembering Him, and so on) are interdependent, and all are bhakti, so in this sense they are 'one'. But while each of the nine forms (nava-lakṣaṇa) of bhakti stand on their own, and by following any of them individually (since souls are usually attracted to one of them, particularly), one can attain perfection in devotion – indeed there are specific examples of this in the scriptures, Mahārāj Parīkṣit attained such perfection by hearing, Śukadev Goswāmī by chanting, and so on – still, taken together, there is a natural sequence, beginning with

hearing about the Lord, and culminating in ātma-nivedana, full self-surrender. At the same time, that very self-surrender is at the root of them all.

So, Śrīla Śrīdhar Mahārāj's statement here that "without kīrtana (chanting), how can there be hearing?" might appear at first to be in reverse order, because chanting the Names and Glories of the Lord is the natural result of first hearing them, rather than vice versa. But he is here simply making the point of their interdependence, and this is only a question of language. After all, the very act of chanting, involves hearing – hearing both what you are chanting, also hearing what you have heard others chanting, before that, on which your chanting is based.

2 George Wilhelm Friedrich Hegel (1770–1831), prominent philosopher in the school of German 'Idealism'. His writings are extremely dense, and can appear complex and abstruse to those without a background in European philosophy. Śrīla Śrīdhar Mahārāj had studied Hegel in his college years, and appreciated his philosophy for what he saw as its affinity with Vaiṣṇava thought. In Hegel's view, the ultimate Truth must be, by definition, the Perfect, the Ideal. (This is also called 'Ideal Realism' – that which is ultimately real, must be the Ideal.)

Śrīla Śrīdhar Mahārāj writes: "Hegel's philosophy is sometimes described as 'panentheism' (which) proposes that God is present in all things, but in contrast to 'pantheism' it affirms that God is also an independent being above and beyond all things. Hegel is also known for Perfectionism. He says that the Absolute is both conditioned and unconditioned combined… According to Hegel, the Absolute is by Itself and for Itself. Hegel also used the German equivalent of the expression 'die to live'. These expressions are very useful for those in the theistic line – if you want to live a progressive life you will have to die as you are. Your ego must be dissolved and then the real inner or finer self will come out. This is a good philosophy to have appeared among the Westerners. The concept of 'die to live' comes in the line of Vaiṣṇavism… Hegel was a very important philosopher, and for a Western thinker his philosophy was very near to that of the Eastern thinkers. In many respects Hegel's philosophy is very close to that of Rāmānuja…"

Hegel's Absolute is not static, but a dynamic Existence, and this also has parallels with Vaiṣṇavism, where the Lord is chit-vilāsa, a dynamic, spiritually variegated Unity. Śrīla Śrīdhar Mahārāj again: "In the philosophy of Kṛṣṇa consciousness, the word 'vilāsa' means playful movement… You may take it to mean that the Absolute is absorbed in play." As a serpent moves in a zig-zag way and in this way makes progress, similarly "The movements of the Absolute are not straight, but crooked… The conception of līlā, the divine Pastimes of the Lord, is something like that. This is similar to Hegel's opinion in which the Truth develops in a crooked way through thesis, antithesis, and synthesis: there is thesis, then its opposite, and then again they unify and create a new thesis, then again antithesis, and a greater harmony in synthesis."

3 "You are quite at home" – that you have no apprehension, no fear. You know – not intellectually but experientially – that all is going on by the will and plan of the Lord, and your own interest is fully known and cared for by the Lord and His own, your loving guardians. 'Home comfort' is an expression Śrīla Śrīdhar Mahārāj often used in this regard.

The English anchoress Julian of Norwich (1343–1416), after a series of visions ('shewings'), spiritual insights granted to her, famously wrote in her book *Revelations*, "All will be well, and all will be well, and every kind of thing shall be well." (In one vision, she was shown the world as no bigger than a nut, resting in God's loving hand. Even the English proverb has it: "God is in His heaven, and all is right with the world.")

4 Śrīla B.S. Govinda Mahārāj sometimes used a phrase which sums up well the meaning here: "Surrender does not mean, 'surrender and lie down'!" It is not uncommon that newcomers to the line of devotional service imagine that falling prostrate at the feet of the

guru at the time of initiation, or thereafter, means they are now a surrendered soul – a 'fait accomplis'. Of course, the very symbolism of such obeisance points to much more than this! Such obeisance is mentioned in *Bhagavad-gītā* (4.34) as praṇipāt, submission – but the verse also talks of relevant enquiry (paripraśna), and rendering service (sevayā), all being parts of true surrender. So surrender is not a 'one-time' event, but an ongoing, increasing movement of self-giving in the heart of the disciple/servitor which will naturally manifest in the form of service to the object of his devotion – the guru, Vaiṣṇava, and the Lord.

Kṛṣṇa consciousness is the path of śaraṇāgati, surrender. Therefore, to understand what this means – not just intellectually, but experientially – is of prime importance to a student of the devotional school. Here, theory and practice are not the same, their difference is as great as seeing some honey in a glass jar, and actually tasting it. Since to be 'surrendered to the Lord' in thought, word, and deed, is the constitutional nature of the living being, this should be, one would think, both natural and easy, yet for the conditioned soul who has wandered so far from Home, it is the most difficult. Easy, and difficult – Śrīla A.C. Bhaktivedānta Swāmī Prabhupāda comments, "One may surrender to the Lord in a moment, or it may take millions of years – it depends upon the attitude of the performer."

In the writings of French foundress and teacher St. Therese Couderc (1805–1885) on this subject of self-abandonment to God, we find: "Perhaps you think that all this is very difficult. If so, you are wrong. There is nothing so easy and so pleasant. It all amounts to doing something generous for once and all, and saying with total sincerity: 'My God, I want to be everything for You, please accept my offering.' Then you have said everything that needs to be said."

But then, she continues: "From then on you must take care to keep your soul in this state. You must not shy away from any little sacrifices that might help you advance in virtue. You must always remember that you have surrendered yourself."

Once the soul is given to the Lord, it is His property, it belongs to Him. Of course, it is already His anyway, so one is only 'returning' to the Lord what is His. But once consciously given, it cannot be 'reclaimed'. This is illustrated in the Pastimes of Śrī Chaitanya Mahāprabhu, as recorded in *Śrī Chaitanya-charitāmṛta, Antya-līlā*, Chapter 4. The great devotee-scholar Sanātan Goswāmī had abandoned his high position and prestige in the government of his day to surrender to the lotus feet of Śrī Chaitanya Mahāprabhu. While travelling through the jungles of Central India, he had caught a virulent disease, and whenever he met Lord Chaitanya, the Lord would always embrace him, careless of his weeping sores, which smeared the Lord's body. Sanātan became depressed about this. He already felt himself as very unqualified and abominable. Though he was from Karnātaka brāhmaṇa lineage, he considered himself nīcha-jāti, of low-birth, because he had worked in the Muslim administration and the Court of Hussain Shāh (1494–1525), who was the ruler of Bengal at that time. (To what extent Sanātan had become 'converted to Islam', as such, is not apparently known, but he had changed his name to Sākara Mallik, and adopted certain Muslim customs, so he would have certainly been seen to have 'lost his caste' and would have been shunned by orthodox Hindu society.)

In any case, Sanātan made a secret plan to commit suicide by throwing himself under the giant wheels of the Ratha-yātrā car when the Deity of Lord Jagannāth left the temple on His famous annual journey. Lord Chaitanya, the omniscient God, knew Sanātan's mind however, and when they next met, He said, "What is this, Sanātan? You have surrendered to Me, therefore your body is now My property, it is not yours to do with as you like. And physical renunciation cannot win Kṛṣṇa – if it were possible to attain Him in this way, I would immediately give up thousands of bodies… So, give up your nonsensical desires, Sanātan, they are not favourable for attaining the Lord's mercy. Simply engage yourself in hearing and chanting about the Lord, and very soon you will attain shelter at His lotus feet."

In this chapter, Śrīla Śrīdhar Mahārāj talks at length on the 'six limbs of surrender', and many times we come across the phrase he uses about what surrender means – to 'die to live'. He also says that the 'activities of devotion' – hearing about the Lord, chanting His Names and Glories, and so on – all of these, without having surrender at their basis, will be merely either empty forms, or, at best, 'good karma' – but not bhakti, devotion.

The student of the Bhagavat or devotional school, will be always alert to try and understand more deeply the meaning, and the way, of 'surrender', from different angles and perspectives: from scripture, from the teacher or guru, from the saints, and from deep inner prayer to the Lord.

St. Therese Cauderc in her writings (as quoted above), further unpacks something of the meaning of self-surrender. She says that the Lord has given us so much, but "human souls fail to do what they should in response to this. They are not generous enough. The main way to follow the path of perfection and holiness is to surrender yourself to our good God." And then, going to the very heart of the matter, she writes: "But what does 'surrender yourself' mean? Although I understand the implication of the two words, I cannot explain them. I only know that they are very accommodating, and cover both present and future. To surrender yourself is more than devoting yourself or giving yourself. It is even more than abandoning yourself to God. Surrendering yourself means dying to everything and to the self. It means no longer being concerned with the self except to make sure that it is always turned towards God. To surrender yourself means no longer looking for your own advantage in anything, either spiritual or temporal. It means not seeking your own satisfaction but only what God wants..." (Adapted and translated from *Le Cenacle: Fondemonts Christologiques et Spiritualite*, [Paris, 1991], and *Prier 15 jours avec Therese Couderc* [Paris, 2005].)

As Therese writes here, surrender means "not seeking your own satisfaction, but only what God wants." And here is the crux: how do we know just what God wants? Could we ever know? Is there any guarantee that we are doing His will, and indeed, not our own? The French Jesuit Jean Pierre de Caussade (d.1751) in the collection of his talks and letters published posthumously as *Abandonment to*

Divine Providence (also sometimes called *The Sacrament of the Present Moment*), says that what comes to us, moment to moment, whatever it may be, is God's will for us, and to respond to that with hope, courage, and perseverance, itself constitutes surrender, and is to do His will.[5] Others like John Cardinal Henry Newman, have said that to discover our specific and unique vocation or 'calling' in life, and to follow that, is to do God's will (see Note 1). But, even accepting all this, still, can we be sure?

Thomas Merton expressed this position well when he writes: "My Lord God, I have no idea where I am going. I do not see the road ahead of me. I cannot know for certain where it will end, nor do I really know myself, and the fact that I think that I am following Your will does not mean that I am actually doing so. But I believe that the desire to please You does in fact please You, and I hope I have that desire in all that I am doing. I hope that I will never do anything apart from that desire, and I know that if I do this, You will lead me by the right road though I may know nothing about it. Therefore will I trust in You always, though I may seem to be lost and in the shadow of death. I will not fear, for You are ever with me and You will never leave me to face my perils alone." (The *Prayer of Thomas Merton*). (See Note 2.)

As is clear from the above, to have faith does not mean not to have doubts, or never to have them. As one savant has put it, "The opposite of faith is not doubt, it is fear." Perhaps even with the best of spiritual help – a good spiritual director, or guru, the backing of scripture and tradition, and association of wise and faithful souls on the path – it is in the human condition itself to experience, at times, weakness and doubt. In his book *Contemplative Hunger*, Professor of Moral Theology and Spiritual Director Fr. Donald Haggerty writes: "Do religious people of high self-confidence somehow imply by their external bearing a spiritual contradiction? Is it possible that one who loves God, and searches intently for Him, can be only full of assurances in all choices? Or is it nearer to the truth that when a soul is closer to God ... there is more likely to be at times a tentativeness, a restlessness, a questioning directed at self, precisely because in the privacy of the soul in its relations with God a loss is continually taking place? This is a loss and stripping of self that can leave the soul groping at times for an answer, unsettled, uncertain of itself, in large part because he is unsure exactly what God is asking of him. Not always, it seems, does the advancement of a soul in relations to God bring immediate courage and clarity and shining lustre. The spiritual life is a journey of varied experiences that include fits and starts and stumbling steps as well as times running with the rush of the wind at one's back. And yet a life truly seeking God is mysteriously of one piece. Nonetheless, the harmonious interplay of contrasting experiences over a lifetime may be recognised only at the end. What we will recognise perhaps is that every impoverishment of our lives opened a path of deeper surrender to God." (pp.93–94)

From the Vaiṣṇava scriptures and teachings, we learn that the full blessings of the Lord come to a soul through their complete surrender – in body, mind and words – and that this is practically effected in the sincere attempt to 'satisfy the Vaiṣṇava', that is, to follow the advice, and to carry out the instructions, of the pure Vaiṣṇava, the devotee. This is, as it were, the 'litmus test', for it may be easy to think or believe one is doing the 'will of God', but it takes greater surrender to serve His servants – the devotees.
To mundane vision the devotee is, after all, a human being, but there is a misconception, a misperception, here. Even in the Christian monastic traditions of both East and West, the vow of obedience calls one to be submissive towards those who are "standing in the place of God" – superiors such as the Prior, or the Abbot, or Mother Superior (and indeed, in degree, to all one's brothers or sisters).
But in the Vedic scriptures, it is stated clearly and uncompromisingly that to satisfy the pure devotee of the Lord is to please the Lord.
He is more satisfied with such service than the attempt to satisfy Him directly, since His pure devotee is very dear to Him. This then is indeed the 'guarantee', if such be sought, that the disciple-soul is truly 'doing the Lord's will', that He is truly being served, at least as far as is possible for him to know, as a conditioned soul.

Śrīla Viśvanāth Chakravartī Ṭhākur therefore sings: "I offer my obeisance unto the lotus feet of Śrī Guru, who is said by all the scriptures to be non-different from the Lord Himself, and is considered to be so by the sādhus (holy persons), yet is the Lord's beloved devotee. Therefore I offer my obeisance to his lotus feet, praising him and meditating on his glory at the three junctions of the day. By his grace, one gains the Lord's grace. Without his grace, one has no shelter anywhere." (*Śrī Śrī Guruvāṣṭakam*, verses 7–8).

5 In the theology of the Christian tradition, there are three 'Cardinal Virtues': Faith, Hope, and Charity, or Love. One writer has helpfully described their inter-relation as being like a plant growing towards God: faith is the seed, hope the stem, and love the flower. But the Virtue of Hope does not mean just a kind of optimism, or hope in the ordinary sense, as meaning "I am not sure, but I hope…". Theologically it means looking forward, with absolute confidence, in the expectation that God will give us everything which is necessary to bring us to the end He has in view for us. And Hope has two parts, or constituents, Courage and Perseverance. In the Vaiṣṇava tradition a similar idea is expressed succinctly in Śrīla Rūpa Goswāmī's *Upadeśāmṛta,* (*The Nectar of Instruction*), in which, in eleven verses, he offers a blueprint of essential principles to be followed if a practitioner is to really advance in Kṛṣṇa consciousness. In verse three, out of six principles 'favourable to the execution of pure devotional service' the first three he gives are: 1, being enthusiastic; 2, endeavouring with confidence; and 3, being patient (utsahān, niśchayād, dhairyāt).

It is Hope, through grace, which brings a soul through all trials and difficulties, with courage and perseverance. In other words, it gives confidence and trust in God. No wonder then, that St. Paul wrote in his letter to the Romans (8,24): "We are saved by hope."

Note 1: John Cardinal Henry Newman (1801–1890) was a convert to the Roman Catholic Church from Anglicanism. Prior to this, he was a leading light in the Oxford Movement which attempted to bring the Church of England back to its patristic roots (the teaching of the early Church Fathers). Theologian and philosopher, Newman wrote several books, hymns (notably *Lead on, Kindly Light*), poems, and plays. His book *Apologia pro vita sua*, a kind of spiritual autobiography written in defence of his beliefs against the criticism of the (Protestant) Charles Kingsley, has become a minor classic. Newman was canonised in 2019.

Note 2: Thomas Merton (1915–1968), American-born Trappist monk, was one of the most prolific and notable Catholic writers of the twentieth century. His personal journals, published posthumously, reveal the depth of thought and insight of this brilliant and somewhat angst-ridden individual who struggled with the paradoxes in his own life. (He never really resolved for example the dichotomy between his strong desire for solitude, as a monk at Gethsemani Abbey, Kentucky, and an equally strong desire to communicate, to interact with the wider world and its issues, through his writings, his vast correspondence with people from all walks of life, and his lectures and talks.)

His books such as *The Seven Storey Mountain* (charting his religious conversion), *Seeds of Contemplation*, *The Sign of Jonas*, *No Man is an Island* and *Conjectures of a Guilty Bystander*, among many others, seem to hold a fascination for continuing generations of spiritual seekers. Merton stands out particularly as a pioneer of inter-religious dialogue. In this he was years ahead of his time (he was writing through the 1950s and 60s). He believed this to be something very natural and healthy, essential even, for the true spiritual seeker. Far from compromising a person's integrity in, or 'chastity' to their own spiritual faith-tradition, he saw that – assuming of course that they were sufficiently firmly rooted in that tradition – it could only enhance it. "Surely we cannot doubt," he writes, "that the values hidden in Oriental thought may be able, if properly grasped and appreciated, to lead us to a deeper and wiser understanding of our own (Christian) magnificent mystical tradition, just as Platonism, without actually 'influencing' the Greek Fathers, gave them a language and a sensibility that were equipped to penetrate in a specially significant way the depths of the revealed mystery of Christ. At least this much can and must be said: the 'universality' and 'catholicity' which are essential to the Church necessarily imply an ability and a readiness to enter into dialogue with all that is pure, wise, profound and humane in every kind of culture. In this sense at least a dialogue with Oriental wisdom becomes necessary…" (From *A Thomas Merton Reader*, ed. Thomas P. McDonnell, New York: *Harcourt, Brace and World*, 1962, pp.302- 3).

Michael Ford, author and religious broadcaster, writing of Merton in his book *Spiritual Masters for All Seasons* (2009), says that in Merton's eyes, genuine dialogue should end not only in communication, but, since the spiritual search is always centred on Love, even in communion, a real joining of hearts, yet with each person remaining faithful to his own religious path. During his lifetime, however, Merton's views in this regard, as well as his uncompromising stand on issues of racial equality, social justice, war, etc., made him often unpopular with the institutional Church hierarchy, who even for a time forbade him to publish. However, like the Church Father Origen, Meister Eckhart, and others before him, his work has stood the test of time, and since his death has enjoyed an ever increasing popularity. (It is said the last four Popes have all read him; but it is unlikely that he will be joining the 10,000 or so canonised saints of the Roman Catholic Church!)

Chapter Fifteen

Devotion – Real and Apparent

The Eye to See Devotion

Question: Since the Vaiṣṇava does not want to exhibit symptoms of devotion, how does one detect the pure Vaiṣṇava, one who is on the highest platform?
Śrīla Śrīdhar Mahārāj: The judgement, the decision, as to who is a Vaiṣṇava, is not by the physical feats – they may be all deception, or imitation.[1] There are other things we can recognise. There must be some intrinsic signs: a real conception about the Absolute, detachment from everything else, and earnestness for service to Him, *bhaktiḥ pareśānubhavo viraktir anyatra.*[2]

When one first enters into the study of a particular science, then he should come to know who is an expert in that science. Initially, however, an artist or a sculptor, cannot know, cannot recognise, the intricacies of that science or its stages of advancement. Similarly, the bona fide student of a particular spiritual school, with the help of an expert, will be able to understand what is what, in that line, that department.

One who is a student of the Bhagavata school must be bona fide, and his study must be in the connection of a true Vaiṣṇava. The standpoint, the angle of vision, to see things properly, must come from that side, from the Vaiṣṇava. And the student's eligibility is śraddhā, faith. That is, bhāgya, auspicious. He has good fortune, sukṛti, *Kṛṣṇa bhāgya iva śraddhā yadi haya*, and because of this he will not think that in his spiritual quest he has come on any 'wild-goose-chase'. Rather, he will think, "O Vaiṣṇava, you have left all the 'concrete' things, all the supposed concrete prospects of this world, and you have come to know that which is almost 'unknowable'. I see that you have spared time, have given sufficient time for this. For what seems so vague, so abstract, so unknowable, you are leaving all the concrete things of enjoyment in the world." And so he will ask, he will enquire of the Vaiṣṇava, "Why have you taken this course? And how, in what way, are you doing so?"

Selection and Elimination

The students of this school are also to be examined, to be tested, and some will be rejected. Just as so many students will send in their application to be admitted in the college, but when they take a general examination, all do not pass; many may be eliminated and a selected few will be accepted for study.

Similarly this is the test of faith. You may have, in a general way, left the so-called concrete things, for the abstract – but for what sort of 'abstract'? What is it that you are searching for? And what mundane touch do you have in your mind in your aspiration for that? That will be examined. In this way there is always selection based on the purity of purpose. "Your ideal, is it high? Is it the highest goal of your life? And how much are you prepared to sacrifice for that? Have you got so much faith in that ideal, that you are ready to become a 'slave', ready for eternal slavery to that? Your addiction to the ideal, the intensity of your reverence, the degree of your dedication to it – is it such that you are ready to pay that price to purchase it?" This will be the test.

The Zonal Visa

One who is living in that plane, that plane of your highest ideal, will come and examine you. And he will give a 'visa' accordingly for you to go from 'door to door'[3] in different zones in the spiritual realm. "With this visa you can go to Vaikuṇṭha." Or, "With this visa – with more sacrifice – you can come to Ayodhyā, to Dwārakā, to Mathurā, to Vṛndāvan…" In this way the zonal visa will be granted to you by examining how far you can render service in such intensity as it is demanded from that particular quarter.

A Positive Serving-life

Mahāprabhu told Sanātan Goswāmī, that for getting devotion of Kṛṣṇa if it is demanded that in a minute or in a second you are to undergo death crores[4] of times, that also is not the proper price:

> **"sanātana, deha-tyāge kṛṣṇa yadi pāiye**
> **koṭi-deha kṣaṇeke tabe chāḍite pāriye"**
> *(Śrī Chaitanya-charitāmṛta: Antya-līlā, 4.55)*

"My dear Sanātan," He said, "if I could attain Kṛṣṇa by committing suicide, I would certainly give up millions of bodies without a moment's hesitation."

Still, for the satisfaction of Kṛṣṇa, if it is necessary that you will have to give up your life, your unit of sacrifice, crores of times, are you ready for that? All our attraction is concentrated in this body; our attraction for enjoyment in this world depends on this body, it is centred there, and even if one is ready to sacrifice this body millions of times, that also may not take us to that domain.[5]

What then is the real standard of sacrifice? We are to begin by considering this point. What kind of sacrifice is real sacrifice? It is not only that we are to dismiss wholesale our attraction for the mundane, but there must be positive appreciation for the serving life. So the advice is, go slowly, but surely, with *śravaṇa-kīrtana.* Your practice of hearing and chanting about the Lord, that is the only path to attain Him, and not by showing your 'heroism' of any mortal type.

Soldiers who are prepared to sacrifice their life, who do not care for physical death, in them also we find a kind of 'surrender', but what for? It is for fame, or in one form or another for some mundane end, but all in the relativity of the mundane world. Or, in the case of insanity – when someone is mad, he does not know what is good or bad – he may act in any way, do anything, and may die. So, both from ignorance or from necessity for mundane ends for mastership or fame, we may find apparent surrender, sacrifice, but all are only connected with this mundane world.

Service of the Vaiṣṇava

Our aspiration to the ideal, the higher ideal in the plane of dedication, and the purity of that aspiration – that is the criterion, and that should be considered to be the unit which is required from us, for our admission there. Such aspiration comes from śraddhā, faith. *Adau śraddhā*, the beginning of the path of surrender is faith. And faith is born from sukṛti, good fortune, and that is independent of us – *ajñāta-sukṛti* – it comes by the grace of the higher world. Devotion, bhakti, cannot be produced by anything mundane, but only bhakti can produce bhakti, *bhaktyā sañjātayā bhaktyā*.[6] Bhakti is ahaituki, causeless. None can produce it, but only bhakti can extend herself – the cause is in the upper world. It cannot but be so because bhakti is not a product of this material world. We are only to try to utilise that fortune, that grace of bhakti, and to serve. So, very cautiously, relying on the Vaiṣṇava, and with the innermost sanction of our heart, we are to try to make progress. We are to surrender to, and to serve to, the Vaiṣṇava. Nothing should be done without the order of a Vaiṣṇava (*Vaiṣṇavera ājñā kāja kari*).

Strict – to the Extreme

There was a disciple of our Guru Mahārāj Śrīla Bhakti Siddhānta Saraswatī Ṭhākur, and on this point, that we won't do anything without the sanction of a Vaiṣṇava, that devotee was so serious. He was so strict on this principle, that many thought it too much, too extreme. On one occasion, he was to go by train with some other Vaiṣṇavas to a certain place. When all the devotees got up on the train, he remained standing on the platform – because no Vaiṣṇava had ordered him to get into the carriage! That disciple's name was Professor Sanyal, Nishikanta Sanyal. He was a good scholar, and the head of examinations at a particular university. He also wrote the book *Śrī Kṛṣṇa Chaitanya* and he was the editor of the *The Harmonist* journal at that time. He had so much adherence to this idea, that, "without the order of a Vaiṣṇava, I won't budge an inch." It was his general motto of life. He gave so much importance to the Vaiṣṇava.

There is another incident with him in this connection that I remember. When the Maṭh was transferred from a rented house to its present location, its own property at Bagbazar, Kolkata, the Deity was carried in a chariot and placed in the new temple. There was an utsava, a festival, and the feeding of the devotees and the public, and we went to our beds at around one o'clock that night. As we had newly entered that house, we all simply took some place there, and spread our beds. My bedding was just beside that of Nishikanta Sanyal.

During the night, he felt at one point that he was dying, and in the morning he told me, very slowly, "Last night, I felt my heart was failing. I thought I should wake you, rouse you, but I knew that you were very much tired, and I should not disturb a Vaiṣṇava in his rest. I thought, 'He has worked hard all day and half the night. He is so tired and he is sleeping, I should not disturb him. Let me see if this crisis will go away.' Anyhow, that crisis has gone, but still I am feeling very weak."

I knew that he was a very serious man, not ordinary, and immediately I told Śrīla Prabhupāda, our Guru Mahārāj, what he had been saying to me, and straight away the doctor was arranged for him.

'Yours is Not The Judgement Seat'

So, that Professor Sanyal was of such serious character – even dying, he does not like to disturb others' sleep! And he won't do anything if not ordered by a Vaiṣṇava. It is an example, though extreme. He was my senior, a little senior, and once he told me, to me particularly, "If I read *Śrīmad Bhāgavatam* or *Chaitanya-*

charitāmṛta of my own accord, it won't be bhakti, it will be karma or jñāna, but if a Vaiṣṇava orders one to go on with the reading, it will be devotion." Do you follow?

Devotee: Yes.

Śrīla Śrīdhar Mahārāj: Otherwise, you are reading to acquire knowledge, and that is not service. To acquire knowledge, to keep your position high, to help you to deliver lectures, to receive appreciation – this is all mundane. But if strictly the whole of your energy will be spent on carrying out the order of a Vaiṣṇava, then it will be service.

So, you are to practise in this way from the beginning, that you are not acting for your own interest but acting on the order of a Vaiṣṇava. And you won't go to occupy the position of a judge in your own case, you are not to be the 'judge of your own crime'. That is, you are not to take part in giving the order, as to in what way you are to utilise your energy. You must be quite disinterested – the order must come from above, and you are to serve it.

Purest Intention

Your energy must be utilised always for the Vaiṣṇavas' interest. And if you make yourself your own judge, you will always give judgement in your own favour. That possibility is there! (Laughter). But we should try to have self-abnegation, to the extreme, and the judgement must come from the other side, from the Vaiṣṇava, whether you are dedicating, or, in the guise of dedicating, you are enjoying, you are out to exploit.

This is a very subtle point, because exploitation in the higher plane may not seem, from the gross plane, to be exploitation at all. And this is difficult to discern, just as a capitalist may give, may spend much money for someone or for some cause, taking it from his own purse, but with the far-sight, the intention, that he will get a thousand times more money in return. So, ostentatious 'self-distribution' is not self-distribution at all. It is not service, not real service. It should be judged from another side, another angle of vision: the intention, how much it is self-centred, or Centre-centred.

Endnotes to Chapter 15

1 Śrīla Śrīdhar Mahārāj is referring to the 'physical feats' in imitation of genuine spiritual symptoms of pure devotion, such as may be manifested in the higher stages – tears, shivering, fainting, and so on – which certain yogīs and sādhus and supposed jīvan-muktas (liberated souls) sometimes project, usually to attract name and fame, followers, etc. Some persons can be quite expert in artificially producing such symptoms – indeed even accomplished film or stage actors can do so – and for the inexperienced, it can be difficult to know or to detect if such things are genuine. A devotee of higher type does not like, however, to publicly show any such symptoms. However they may on occasion spontaneously or uncontrollably manifest physically due to their overflowing, ecstatic inner condition of love for Kṛṣṇa.

2 **bhaktiḥ pareśānubhavo viraktir**
anyatra chaiṣa trika eka-kālaḥ
prapadyamānasya yathāśnataḥ syus
tuṣṭiḥ puṣṭiḥ kṣud-apāyo 'nu-ghāsam

"Devotion, direct experience of the Supreme Lord, and detachment from other things – these three occur simultaneously for one who has taken shelter of the Supreme Personality of Godhead, in the same way that pleasure, nourishment and relief from hunger come simultaneously and increasingly, with each bite, for a person engaged in eating."

3 From 'door to door, in different zones' – the soul who has been granted a 'visa' to go to a particular spiritual plane, can then move freely within that realm.

4 100,000 = 1 lakh. 100 lakhs = 1 crore (10 million). A lot of births!

5 The divine abode of eternal service to Kṛṣṇa.

6 *Śrīmad Bhāgavatam*: 11.3.31.

Chapter Sixteen

The Real Standard of Sacrifice

Don't Be A Make-Believer

Śrī Chaitanya Mahāprabhu said,

> **na prema-gandho 'sti darāpi me harau**
> **krandāmi saubhāgya-bharaṁ prakāśitum**[1]

What standard of sacrifice is shown here? Mahāprabhu says, "I am crying, shedding tears so much – but it is only for fame, 'O just see, I have so much love for Kṛṣṇa!' Only to attract people towards Me, I am shedding tears. It is all artificial."

Mahāprabhu has raised the standard of sacrifice, the standard of real devotion, so high. And we are to think, "Where are we? What does this mean for us?"

So, don't be a make-believer! Śrīla Bhakti Vinod Ṭhākur has expressed in his song *Prārthanā Lālasāmayī* the mood of a genuine devotee:

> **kṛpa kara vaiṣṇava ṭhākura**
> **sambandha jāniyā, bhajite bhajite,**
> **abhimāna hau dūra**
> **'āmi ta vaiṣṇava', e buddhi haile,**
> **amānī nā ha'ba āmi**
> **pratiṣṭhāsā āsi', hṛdaya dūṣibe,**
> **haiba nirayagāmī**
> **tomāra kinkara, āpane jāniba,**
> **'guru'- abhimāna tyaji'**

tomāra uchiṣṭha, padajala-reṇu,
sadā niṣkapaṭe bhaji
'nije sreṣṭha' jāni', uchiṣṭādi dāne,
habe abhimāna bhāra
tāi śiṣya tava, thākiyā sarvvadā,
nā laiba pūjā kā'ra
amānī mānada, haile kīrttane
adhikāra dibe tumi
tomāra charaṇe, niṣkapaṭe āmi,
kāṅdiyā luṭiba bhūmi

"Please give your mercy to me now, O revered pure devotee! O Vaiṣṇava Ṭhākur! Then only my false ego will go far away by my constant worship in full knowledge of my real, eternal position. If I falsely think that 'I am a Vaiṣṇava', then I shall look forward to receiving respect from others. And if the desire for fame and reputation pollutes my heart, then certainly I shall go to live in hell instantly. Renouncing the false conception that 'I am a guru', I will understand myself to be your humble servant. I sincerely worship the remnants of your food, O pure devotee, as well as the water that has washed the sacred dust of your lotus feet. By giving others the remnants of my food, I shall consider myself superior and shall be burdened with the weight of false pride. Therefore, always remaining your surrendered disciple, I shall not accept worship from anyone. If you will bestow upon me the capacity to chant the Holy Name, I will then give all honour to others without expecting any respect for myself. Thus I will sincerely weep in ecstasy while rolling on the ground at your lotus feet."

We are always to live in the relativity of the spiritual master as 'Vaiṣṇava dāsa', servant of the Vaiṣṇava. Then whatever we do, anything and everything will be only on the order of the

Vaiṣṇava, the superior. Always we must connect ourself with some higher 'dictator'.[2] If we go on in this way, always living with this principle, we will be safe: "I am not doing any duty independently but under the guidance of a Vaiṣṇava." We must develop this sort of attitude sincerely within us. Our 'original thinking', independent thinking, must be buried for good.[3] So, don't be a make-believer, a self-deceiver!

But at the same time, we must not be afraid. Kṛṣṇa assures Arjuna:

na hi kalyāṇa-kṛt kaśchid
durgatiṁ tāta gachchhati[4]

"A person who performs virtuous actions, O dear one, never suffers an ill-fate." If I do not deceive myself, then none can deceive me. The purity, the quality, and not the quantity, in the surrender, the way of surrender, that is what is important. To surrender more and more to the Lord, that is self-determination, and it means to 'die to live', because everything is for Him – otherwise, He cannot be Absolute. I am searching for the Absolute, and everything is for Him, that Absolute. I must submit to this law, faithfully, that everything is for Him, and we also are for Him, and not that He is for us.

The Lie in The Half-Truth

The impersonalists, māyāvādīs, cannot flourish here in this truth, this reality. When confronted with it, they want to enter into the 'prison-cell' of mukti, liberation, and that is like suicide. They can't tolerate that everything is for Him, and that we are also for Him.

That this material world, that 'all we survey'[5], is not for us, this much they can find out – that we cannot thrive here in the plane of exploitation and reaction, in the campaign that 'everything is for me'. They can discover this clearly, but they conclude that, "Nothing is for me – so I must go and enter into a 'suicide-cell'." But that there is something more, a Higher Reality, and that everything is for Him, and I am also for Him – they can't accommodate into their brain this broad idea. That is the difference between the jñānī and the Vaiṣṇava. The jñānī can realise that we cannot thrive in the mortal environment. This much, the negative side, they can grasp. But the positive side, the optimistic side – the Lord is there, and everything is for Him, and not for me, and only there in that plane, in that land, I can thrive – this they cannot understand.

The Fullest Engagement

To 'die to live', to sacrifice oneself for this high ideal, is real self-determination, it is svarūpa-siddhi.[6] Mukti, liberation proper, means this. And death means not only of the flesh, but of the sūkṣma-deha, the internal subtle body of its different layers. Then further, within consciousness itself, the chitta, there are many different layers. There is the Vaikuṇṭha conception, the Dwārakā conception, and we are to pass through these layers of the purely spiritual plane also, and enter into the Vṛndāvan conception of Kṛṣṇa. In this way our risk, and our surrender, will increase more and more. Our sacrifice must be wholesale, and then we will find our part in the mādhurya-rasa, the conjugal relation with the Lord, the twenty-four hours per day engagement. Only there, is such engagement possible, and that is the highest. Even service in vātsalya-rasa, the relation of a guardian of the Lord, cannot give this. To say so may seem very harsh, cruel,[7] but it is so. It is mentioned in the śāstra, and we also may be able to have some conjecture, some idea about it.[8]

In mādhurya-rasa in Dwārakā in svakīya, conjugal relationship, there also this wholesale twenty-four hours engagement is not present. It is only to be found in Vṛndāvan.[9] And it is peculiar to the nature of the parakīya relationship there, that though meeting, union, with Kṛṣṇa is not always possible, not available always,[10] the internal intensity of those paramours is so great that even in the separation, there is union. Their heart is so drawn to Kṛṣṇa, they are so much thickly and intensely mixed, inter-mixed with Him, that even separation cannot dismiss, cannot do away with, union.

(Śrīla Śrīdhar Mahārāj pauses, and then softly sings:)

rādhe jaya jaya mādhava-dayite
gokula-taruṇī-maṇḍala-mahite...[11]

("O Rādhā! O beloved of Mādhava! O You who are worshipped by all the young girls of Gokula! All glories unto You! All glories unto You!")

(Then, Śrīla Śrīdhar Mahārāj sings:)

yadi, gaura nā ha'ta, tabe ki ha-ita,
kemane dharitām de
rādhāra mahimā prema-rasa-sīmā
jagate jānāta ke?[12]

("If Lord Gaurāṅga had not come to this world, then what would have become of us? How could we have maintained our lives? If He had not come, then how could we ever know of the glories of Śrī Rādhā, and the highest extents of ecstatic love for Kṛṣṇa?")

Our Most Loving Lord

What is devotion? Devotion means love, and love means the highest sacrifice, self-forgetfulness in the service of Kṛṣṇa, Who can draw the most, attract the most. And to attain such a plane of complete self-sacrifice and self-forgetfulness in the service of the Divinity, that is the stage of perfection. Kṛṣṇa is the cause of everything, and everything is meant for Him. He is the Reality, and Reality is by Itself and for Itself – this is a simple statement, a very 'small sound', but infinite meaning is within it.

Kṛṣṇa says:

ahaṁ hi sarva-yajñānāṁ bhoktā cha prabhur eva cha

"I alone am the enjoyer and rewarder of all sacrifices."[13]

Kṛṣṇa is 'Hari', the Lord of all sacrifices, *sarva-yajñeśvara Hari'*. And if you realise this, you will find real peace. Kṛṣṇa says:

bhoktāraṁ yajña-tapasāṁ
sarva-loka-maheśvaram
suhṛdaṁ sarva-bhūtānāṁ
jñātvā māṁ śāntim ṛchchhati[14]

"I am not a cruel king, but I am friendly to you. I am all-in-all, but I am friendly to you all, don't forget this." You are to adjust with this fact, then only can you get peace, real peace. When you come to this fact, this truth, when you adjust to this, then you will get peace. "O, my interest is represented in the Absolute Controller of everything in this world! Why should I worry or bother?[15] Why should I be apprehensive or fearful? And if it is necessary, and if I get the chance, I shall go to promote Him, to make His hand strong,[16] to help His work – and that is service. I am fortunate if He utilises me in any form of service." This is to enter the current, the Absolute current of the world, and it is progressive, it is real progress. But, we are in the 'opposition party'. We form an opposition party to the Absolute current. We want to create our separate current in our separate kingdom. With this idea we also combine with others and then we clash with different currents of different units in the world here. But to join in the Absolute current, to be an agent of that current, that is what is necessary for us, for peace and harmony, and for the fulfilment of our life.

Endnotes to Chapter 16

1 **na prema-gandho 'sti darāpi me harau**
krandāmi saubhāgya-bharaṁ prakāśitum
vaṁśī-vilāsy-ānana-lokanaṁ vinā
bibharmi yat prāṇa-pataṅgakān vṛthā
(Śrī Chaitanya-charitāmṛta: Madhya-līlā, 2.45)

(Śrī Chaitanya Mahāprabhu said,) "My dear friends, I have not the slightest tinge of love of Godhead within My heart. When you see Me crying in separation, I am just falsely exhibiting a demonstration of My great fortune. Indeed, not seeing the beautiful face of Kṛṣṇa playing His flute, I continue to live My life like an insect, without purpose."

2 The nomenclature 'dictator' has in common parlance evolved a negative connotation, to mean a tyrant, one who rules and treats people despotically, controlling and suppressing them through a totalitarian state, etc… Here it is used in its simple meaning of one who 'dictates to', or directs, his disciples in service, who guides them spiritually. It is a loving guidance. Śrīla Śrīdhar Mahārāj often used the phrases 'a loving guardian' and 'the guardian's loving eye is over us' – the spiritual master is indeed the real friend and well-wisher of the disciple. His guidance, even when it manifests as

'tough love', painful for the disciple because it cuts at and cuts out the promptings of the 'false self', the egoistic self, in him, is coming from his love, not from false ego. This is, by definition, the genuine guru.

The guru's mood is actually one of gratitude to the disciple. He is helping the disciples in their service to the Lord, and he feels that the Lord has sent them to him, to help him in his own service. If, sometimes for the necessary correction of a student who is acting improperly, or heading in the wrong direction, practising or understanding or preaching incorrect siddhānta (established perfect scriptural conclusions), he has to chastise him, that 'chastising mood' of a superior, a master, is the 'guru-abhimāna', a particular mood which descends within him temporarily by the will of the Lord for this purpose. It was said of Śrīla Bhakti Siddhānta Saraswatī Ṭhākur that he was as 'hard as a thunderbolt, soft as a rose' – soft to the devotees, hard to the God-haters, atheists, offenders, etc.

We see in the form of Lord Nārāyaṇa in His four hands, differently placed according to the particular divine 'expansion', the lotus (padma), and conch (śaṅkha) for blessing the devotees, and the fire-wheel (chakra), and mace (gadā), for chastising and killing the demons. The Lord, being the Absolute Truth, is the possessor of all potencies and the Lord of all 'opulences', which have been delineated in the scriptures as wealth, strength, fame, beauty, knowledge, and renunciation (ṣaḍ-aiśvarya). He thus possesses complete vairāgya, detachment, and is equally disposed to all souls, who are spiritual parts and parcels of His energy, without particular attachment to any. At the same time, however, He is attached to those who love Him – His devotees – so much so that He Himself says He has no independence from them, is obliged to them, and is under their control. We see this exhibited by the Lord in His līlā, His Pastimes.

As Śrī Chaitanya Mahāprabhu, He showed extreme attachment for His devotees, but also on occasion, apparently complete detachment, even indifference. In any case, as the Advaya-jñāna, the Absolute Truth, or 'undivided spiritual substantial Reality', His action, whether 'saving' (the devotees), or 'killing' (the demons) is the same, in the sense that whomsoever He touches becomes, by that contact, completely purified, free from all sin, all karma, and thus, liberated. But the liberation of the demons – merging into the Lord's body or into His effulgence – and that of the devotees – attainment of eternal residence and service in the Lord's personal abode – are different.

Actually, Kṛṣṇa – the original Supreme Lord (Svayam Bhagavān) and the origin of all Viṣṇu (Nārāyaṇa) expansions – is engaged in His Pastimes in Goloka Vṛndāvan. The Pastimes of 'killing demons' and 'saving devotees' is a function of His expansion as Viṣṇu. In *Bhagavad-gīṭā*, Kṛṣṇa says that He appears in the world whenever dharma is sufficiently disturbed, to protect the devotees and remove the miscreants (*Bhagavad-gītā: 4.7–8*). It is the Viṣṇu aspect, or function, of Kṛṣṇa Who carries out this task. In Goloka – the higher sphere of the spiritual world, Kṛṣṇa's eternal abode – there are no demons, only rumours of them!

3 This advice surely appears counter-cultural to modern thinking, where a 'rugged individualism' and full 'independence' of thought and action is valued and praised so highly, especially in modern Western or 'first-world' cultures. But such independence, when separated, disconnected, from the Lord and His service, is ultimately not only useless, but being karma-generating, is also spiritually injurious. However, when an individual's powers of independent or 'original' thinking, as well as sensual and physical action (or his thinking, feeling and willing) are utilised in the service of the Lord, the spiritual master, and the devotees – Hari, Guru, Vaiṣṇava – this is in harmony with the Absolute, Who is in Śrīla Śrīdhar Mahārāj's frequent expression, an 'Organic Whole'. This is indeed their actual purpose and their glory, *hṛṣīkeṇa Hṛṣīkeśa-sevanaṁ bhaktir uchyate* (*Bhakti-rasāmṛta-sindhu:* 1.1.12). The senses are to be utilised in service to the master of the senses, Lord Hṛṣīkeśa, Kṛṣṇa.

Catholic monk and author Thomas Merton (1915–1968) writes of the inevitable imbalance, and ultimately chaos, which results when the individual, rather than God, is made the 'centre' of all things:

"The aggressive and dominative view of reality places, at the centre, the individual with its bodily form, its feelings and emotions, its appetites and needs, its loves and hates, its actions and reactions. All these are seen as forming together a basic and indubitable reality to which everything else must be referred, so that all other things are also estimated in their individuality, their actions and reactions, and all the ways in which they impinge upon the interests of the individual self. The world is then seen as a multiplicity of conflicting and limited beings, all enclosed in the limits of their own individuality, all therefore complete in a perfect and vulnerable incompleteness, all seeking to find a certain completeness by asserting themselves at the expense of others, dominating and using others. The world becomes, then, an immense conflict in which the only peace is that which is accorded to the victory of the strong, and in order to taste the joy of this peace, the weak must submit to the strong and join them in their adventures so that they may share in their power."
(From *Choosing to Love the World*, Sounds Time Inc., 2008, p.22)

Note: It is of course highly debatable, as to how much any thought or action is actually 'original' or 'independent', in any case, since in the conditioned world, most behaviour is learned from others, or in some other way downloaded into the consciousness from some already existing plane.

In the Old Testament, we hear from the *Book of Ecclesiastes* (which, like the *Book of Proverbs* which immediately precedes it, is full of pithy, sutra-like wisdom) that indeed, there is 'nothing new under the Sun': "What has been will be again, what has been done will be done again; there is nothing new under the Sun. Is there anything of which one can say, 'Look! This is something new.'? It was here already long ago, it was here before our time." (*Ecc.* 1,9–10 NIV). It is commonly said, "times change", but it seems everything follows a cyclic rather than linear order – and man's conditioned nature remains as it is. This was well known to the sages of old!

[4] *Bhagavad-gītā*: 6.40

[5] From the phrase Śrīla Śrīdhar Mahārāj often used: 'to be the monarch of all we survey'.

[6] *Svarūpa-siddhi*: the 'perfected, true, and eternal self'. Intrinsic here is the soul's eternal function or service, because in the spiritual, absolute world, which is a non-dualistic and yet variegated plane, form and function are one. In the material world, obviously, this is not the case.

[7] Seeming 'harsh or cruel', that is, to souls situated in rasas (serving-relationships with the Lord) other than mādhurya-rasa. Why so? This can be understood by considering the nature of the five primary rasas, which the soul may have with the Lord, seeing from both subjective and objective viewpoints. In 'ascending' order they are: first peacefulness, or neutrality, (śānta rasa); then servitorship (dāsya); friendly (sakhya); parental (vātsalya), and conjugal (mādhurya). Each successive relation includes the qualities of the previous one, but in addition possesses its own special quality. Thus, dāsya-rasa, servitorship, includes the qualities of the neutral relationship – a peaceful or passive appreciation of, and adherence to, the Lord – but with the quality of positive service added. Then after dāsya, servitorship, there is sakhya, friendship, which includes the qualities of both passivity and of service, but with intimacy added such that the 'gap' between servant and master is crossed. For example, the cow-herding boy friends of Kṛṣṇa feel themselves equal to Him. In parental or vātsalya relation, this intimacy is increased further into ever more intense feelings of protectiveness and possessiveness. Those devotees think Kṛṣṇa to be dependent upon them for His life and well-being. And the mādhurya, or conjugal, rasa includes the qualities of all the other relationships but with the addition of its own unique quality. (In relations between lovers, there is sometimes peaceful co-existence, sometimes service,

there is friendship, also protectiveness, as well as conjugal relation itself). Mādhurya-rasa is thus called mukhya-rasa, the all-inclusive relationship, and ādi-rasa, the original. So from this calculation, conjugal rasa is the supreme and highest relationship, the most full and complete engagement opportunity for the soul, in her every aspect, with the Lord.

Subjectively, however, every soul in whatever rasa they are situated is completely satisfied therein because it is their own, eternal, perfected relationship with the Lord. They are playing their own unique part in the Lord's Pastimes in the 'Organic Whole', and that is perfect. Thus for them – those situated in relationships other than conjugal – to hear that, "Only mādhurya-rasa gives twenty-four hours engagement", may sound harsh or cruel. Is their engagement in service, friendship, or parenthood, less than that? Can we think for example, that Hanumān, the great servant of Lord Rāmachandra, the very icon of servitorship itself, is lacking in this regard? And it is also unthinkable that Hanumānjī could desire any other relationship with the Lord than as His servant, eternally. And still, from the 'objective' viewpoint, the fullest, in Śrīla Śrīdhar Mahārāj's words, 'twenty-four hour engagement' is only possible in mādhurya-rasa.

Śrīla A.C. Bhaktivedānta Swāmī Prabhupāda in his writings would harmonise the subjective and objective consideration with the expression, 'perfect, more perfect, most perfect'. In the spiritual world everything is, by very definition, perfect, and yet there is still, inconceivably, gradation – 'more perfect', then 'most perfect' – with mādhurya-rasa, in this context, being the 'most-perfect'. This is what Śrīla Śrīdhar Mahārāj would term 'relativity in the Absolute' – a concept which the impersonalists, or māyāvādīs, "can never accommodate into their brain!"

Note: It is seen in the śāstras that sometimes the Lord Himself, encouraging His devotees in their various relationships with Him, praises their service as 'the best', declaring, "No one can satisfy Me as much as you can." In practical terms, for those who are engaged in the practice of devotional service, all services are, as

Śrīla A.C. Bhaktivedānta Swāmī Prabhupāda would say, 'absolute', since even while still in the world their aim is to satisfy, through Guru and Vaiṣṇava, the Lord, the Absolute. In this sense, it is the case that to sweep the floor of the Lord's temple or to cook for Him in the kitchen is not less than to 'directly' worship Him in His Deity-Form on the altar – or indeed, to preach or distribute books about Him in the street, or any other services. When he would visit the various Temples of his ISKCON society around the world, Śrīlā Prabhupāda would praise the devotees. To those servicing Śrī Śrī Rukmiṇī-Dwārakādīśa in Los Angeles he would say, "O, your Deities are the most beautiful", in London, "O, your Rādhā-Londonīśvara, they are the best!", and so on.

[8] i.e. with the background of scriptural basis for this principle, yet utilising our own God-given reasoning and intelligence, we can get some understanding of how only in mādhurya-rasa can there be the fullest 'twenty-four hour engagement'.

It is understood from the scripture, that as the material world is a 'perverted reflection' of the spiritual world, so also are the relationships found within it, which as we have mentioned are essentially five-fold: neutral, service, friendship, parenthood and intimate. In the upside-down reflection of a tree found in a still lake, the highest part of the real tree is in the lowest position in the reflection. Similarly the highest, most elevated and fullest rasa of amorous-love, specifically of the parakīya (paramour, unmarried) kind, in spiritual reality, is seen in the reflection to be the lowest, degraded position. (All other rasas are, then, graded accordingly, with their counterparts such that in the material world, the condition of śānta, peacefulness and detachment, is the highest attainment, generally; whereas that is but the foundational, beginning, stage in the spiritual reality.) Thus in the material world, the divine amorous love of Kṛṣṇa is reflected as kāma or lust – the two appearing similar but being of opposite quality. As iron and gold are both metals but of 'opposite' quality, so the quality of prema and kāma are opposite – self-giving, and selfishness, respectively.

Śrīla Śrīdhar Mahārāj expressed it succinctly: they are of 'distant similarity, but categorical difference'. As the conjugal relation gives the most complete spiritual engagement for the soul in the spiritual world, so the effects of lust as manifested in sexuality and sexual relations in the material realm, certainly constitute the strongest and most binding aspect of the illusory energy, māyā, to which all conditioned souls are subject – hence the caution in dealing with this aspect of the sensory world, which has been advised by all genuine scriptures and saints.

Lust, as the conditioned soul who becomes its victim knows too well, has an all-enticing and all-encompassing attraction, engaging and overwhelming mind and body and all the senses, to the point of complete absorption, reducing the consciousness to a point, to the elimination of all other considerations, even sometimes of the approach of disaster, or even death. (There are graphic examples in the scripture, such as in the *Mahābhārata*, of this!) Ultimately, only the fullest engagement of the conditioned souls in the practice of Kṛṣṇa consciousness, in association with and under the guidance of true saints, is the remedy for this – proving the truth of the principle that 'a negative can only be replaced by a positive'.

Scripture tells us, and practical experience confirms it, that those spiritual paths which attempt complete withdrawal from the sense-world through the practice of abnegation and renunciation, penances, etc., without this positive engagement, and the consequent attachment to the Names, Forms, Qualities, Associates and Pastimes of the Supreme Lord which it engenders, such paths of renunciation, though they may give temporary relief, ultimately fail.

[9] Referred to here are the two aspects of mādhurya-rasa, conjugal relationship, which a perfected soul may have with Kṛṣṇa: svakīya and parakīya, corresponding to the līlā (Pastimes) of the Lord in Dwārakā and Vṛndāvan respectively.

In Dwārakā city, Kṛṣṇa is a kṣatriya prince of the royal order, the son of Vasudev and Devakī, and is married, by simultaneous independent expansions, to 16,108 queens, each of whom has their own palace, servants, and accoutrements. Kṛṣṇa's relationship to the queens is 'sva-kīya', 'according to the law', according to the religious and social scriptural codes on appropriate behaviour for the married state.

In Vṛndāvan, however, Kṛṣṇa is a gopa, a cow-herding boy of the mercantile (vaiśya) community and caste, who move from place to place in the fields and forests grazing cows and producing milk products for use and selling – a simple, rural life without the sophistications and prestige of city life. This Gopāl-Kṛṣṇa, foster son of Nanda and Yaśodā, is the summum bonum, the most ultimate manifestation of God: the Supreme Lord, in His Nara-līlā, 'humanlike-Pastimes'. It is here we find His amorous Pastimes with the gopīs (the milkmaids of Vṛndāvan), the Pastimes of parakīya-mādhurya-rasa, paramour love.

In these Pastimes the girls have husbands, but their exclusive attachment to Kṛṣṇa is such that forsaking social and religious codes they go to satisfy Kṛṣṇa, their beloved. This spontaneous, unalloyed love for Kṛṣṇa, the Absolute Truth and Absolute Good, represents the highest form of loving service opportunity for the soul, and because it means the wholesale sacrifice of one's life, reputation, prospects – everything – it is most pleasing to Kṛṣṇa. The exchange of love between the gopīs and Kṛṣṇa is on the platform of prema, purely spiritual love, and has nothing to do with material bodies, lust, etc.

Śrī Chaitanya Mahāprabhu, Kṛṣṇa Himself assuming the form and duties of a sannyāsī, monk of the renounced order, worshipped this gopī-bhāva, the service-mood of the gopīs, as the covetable ideal of all spiritual attainments.

10 i.e. because meeting, union with Kṛṣṇa, is more available and possible in the svakīya conjugal relation of the married state.

11 This is the refrain in the bhajan (hymn) *Śrī Rādhikā-stava* composed by the great devotee and spiritual successor of Śrī Chaitanya Mahāprabhu, Śrīla Rūpa Goswāmī. It is part of his compilation *Stava-mālā*. It is traditionally sung in Gauḍīya Vaiṣṇava

Temples on Rādhāṣṭamī, the Appearance day of Śrīmatī Rādhārāṇī, to honour Her. The chorus (*Rādhe, jaya jaya Mādhava dayite*) is sung between each of these three verses:

dāmodara-rati-vardhana-veśe
hari-niṣkuṭa-vṛndā-vipineśe

vṛṣabhānūdadhi-nava-śaśi-lekhe
lalitā-sakhi guṇa-ramita-viśākhe

karuṇām kuru mayi karuṇā-bharite
sanaka-sanātana-varṇita-charite

"O You Who dress Yourself in such a way as to increase Lord Dāmodara's love and attachment for You! O Queen of Vṛndāvan, which is the pleasure grove of Lord Hari! O new moon Who has arisen from the ocean of King Vṛṣabhānu! O friend of Lalitā! O You Who make Viśākhā loyal to You due to Your wonderful qualities of friendliness, kindness, and faithfulness to Kṛṣṇa! O You Who are filled with compassion! O You Whose divine characteristics are described by the great sages Sanaka and Sanātan! O Rādhā please be merciful to me!"

[12] This is the first verse of a song composed by Śrīla Vāsudev Ghoṣa, a dear devotee of Śrī Chaitanya Mahāprabhu known for his sweet singing (kīrtana), in which he expresses his extreme appreciation for, and wonder at, the merciful appearance of the Lord. The song is simply titled after the first line, *Jadi Gaura nā ha'ta* – "If Gaura had not come." The remaining verses, translated from their Bengali, run as follows:

(2) Who would have had the capacity to render ecstatic devotional service, following the mood of the damsels of Vraja? Indeed, the clever expertise of the Vraja-gopīs is essential for entering the supremely sweet forest of Vṛndā, Śrī Vṛndāvan.

(3) Sing again and again the wonderful qualities of Lord Gaurāṅga while keeping your heart simple. In the ocean of this

material world, not a single person has ever seen such a magnanimous and merciful Lord.

(4) Even though I am chanting 'Gaurāṅga!' somehow I have not melted in ecstatic love. So, how have I maintained the burden of this body? How is it that the creator has given this Vāsu, a stone in place of his heart?

13 *Bhagavad-gīta*, 9.24:

ahaṁ hi sarva-yajñānāṁ
bhoktā cha prabhur eva cha
na tu mām abhijānanti
tattvenātaś chyavanti te

"I alone am the enjoyer and rewarder of all sacrifices, but being ignorant of My position, the demigod worshippers fall to take birth again."

14 *Bhagavad-gītā*, 5.29:

bhoktāraṁ yajña-tapasāṁ
sarva-loka-maheśvaram
suhṛdaṁ sarva-bhūtānāṁ
jñātvā māṁ śāntim ṛchchhati

"I am the enjoyer and objective of the sacrifices performed by persons of action, and of the austerities performed by persons of knowledge. I am Nārāyaṇa, the indwelling monitor of all planes of life, the worshipable Supreme Personality who awards liberation. I am Kṛṣṇa, the well-wisher of all, and the dear friend of the devotees. One who knows Me thus, attains the bliss of knowing his own original identity."

Note: Śrīla Śrīdhar Mahārāj in his rendition of *Bhagavad-gītā – The Hidden Treasure of the Sweet Absolute* has not given individual commentaries on each verse, as has been done by many scholars in their editions, notably Śrīla A.C. Bhaktivedānta Swāmī Prabhupāda in his *Bhagavad-gītā As It Is*. Śrīla Śrīdhar Mahārāj has only commented on certain 'key' verses separately (for example, the chatuḥ-ślokī, the four seed verses of the *Gītā*: 10.8–11), especially where their significance has been noted by previous Āchāryas such as Śrīla Jīva Goswāmī, Śrīla Bhakti Vinod Ṭhākur, Śrīla Viśvanāth Chakravarti, etc. He has, rather, mostly given in-depth extended translations to the verses, as can be clearly seen here in his treatment of *Bhagavad-gītā*: 5.29.

It is worth offering here also the translation of this verse by Śrīla A.C. Bhaktivedānta Swāmī Prabhupāda which highlights succinctly the three points it makes, namely that Kṛṣṇa is

- The Enjoyer (bhoktāraṁ yajña-tapasāṁ)
- The Controller or Lord of all (sarva-loka-maheśvaram), and
- The Friend of all (suhṛdaṁ sarva-bhūtānāṁ)

– and that the knowledge of this, can give one real peace in life.

Śrīla Prabhupāda translates this verse in this way: "One who knows Me as the Enjoyer of all sacrifices and austerities, the Supreme Lord of all planets and demigods, and the benefactor and well-wisher of all living entities, attains peace from the pangs of material miseries."

In 1966, after the registration of his ISKCON society in New York, Śrīla Prabhupāda wrote a pamphlet based on this important verse, which was widely distributed by his disciples, entitled *The Peace Formula*. Its gist was, as said, that simply by knowing God, Kṛṣṇa, to be the Enjoyer and the Controller, but also one's best and closest friend (He is living in everyone's heart, as Paramātmā) – and, most importantly, the organising of society, individually and collectively, to act in accordance with this knowledge – this is the only possible formula for peace in the world, individually, socially, nationally, internationally, and universally. Joining NATO, United Nations, or any other human construct or institution, though well-intended, will ultimately fail because it ignores God (though perhaps nominally claiming 'In God We Trust'). This explanation no doubt sounds too simplistic to the ears of the modern 'civilised' man, but it is, as Śrīla Prabhupāda repeated often, nevertheless the fact.

15 "Why should I worry, or bother uselessly trying to extract, to wrest my 'own interest' from this world, or feel fearful or apprehensive when/if I fail to do so? All my real interests are fully taken care of in the service to the Lord."

16 "To make His hand strong in the world" – to try to help, to be an instrument, in establishing the 'reign of God (Kṛṣṇa) in the world', to make people aware of Him, His beauty and sweetness, and not just as the Creator and Controller, but as Friend – in general, to work to make all people conscious of God, to be God conscious, Kṛṣṇa conscious.

Note: It is understood that Kṛṣṇa can of course effect all of this Himself by His simple wish alone, but He likes to use His devotees as His 'instruments' – and this, to their glory. In *Bhagavad-gītā*, just before the onset of battle in the great Kurukṣetra war, Kṛṣṇa said to Arjuna, that by His own arrangements all the soldiers present there were already slain, and that he, Arjuna, would be but His instrument to achieve this:

tasmāt tvam uttiṣṭha yaśo labhasva
jitvā śatrūn bhuṅkṣva rājyaṁ samṛddham
mayaivaite nihatāḥ pūrvam eva
nimitta-mātraṁ bhava savya-sāchin
(Śrīmad Bhagavad-gītā: 11.33)

"So, arise! Be glorious! Conquer the enemies and enjoy a flourishing kingdom. All these warriors have already been killed by Me. O Savya-sāchin, you be but an instrument."

In this way, while the devotee may receive glory, or name and fame, for his achievements, he does not become puffed-up, proud, because he well knows that Kṛṣṇa is really the 'doer'.

In *Bhagavad-gītā*, Kṛṣṇa reiterates this in several places: He is *pauruṣaṁ nṛṣu*, the ability (lit: masculinity) in man (7.8); *buddhir buddhimatām asmi, tejas tejasvinām aham*, "I am the intelligence of the intelligent, the power of the powerful" (7.10); *balaṁ balavatāṁ chāhaṁ*, "I am the strength of the strong, without selfishness and attachment" (7.11); *tejas tejasvinām aham, jayo 'smi vyavasāyo 'smi, sattvaṁ sattvavatām aham,* "I am the glory of the glorious, I am victory, I am perseverance, and I am the power of truth of the honest" (10.36). And then, we have Kṛṣṇa's beautiful admission in 10.34:

kīrtiḥ śrīr vāk cha nārīṇāṁ
smṛtir medhā dhṛtiḥ kṣamā

"Of the feminine qualities I am fame, beauty, perfect speech, remembrance, intelligence, patience and forgiveness – the seven wives of Dharma."

Chapter Seventeen

Absolute Harmony

Autocratic Absolute

The Absolute is not under any law. He is an Autocrat. Whatever is against His will, is objectionable; and of those objectionable things, there may be thousands and more – because He to Whom those 'offences' may be committed is infinite! He is not under any law. To think that He is so, to become fixed in such a conception about Him, and to think that we ourselves must always follow this idea in our relation to Him, that is for the beginners. They should do so, but as much as one will make progress, as much as he will be nearer to Him, to that Autocratic Subject, to the Lord, he will know what is His sweet will, and what is not, and he will do accordingly.

In this way there is development, progress, and adjustment. For the primary class, the beginners, most important is the 'law', the śāstra. In the middle stage, it is the will of His agents – whatever is not approved by the guru and the Vaiṣṇava should be avoided. And in the highest stage, in relation to the Absolute, the whimsical Absolute, whatever He wants, that is what must be supplied, and whatever He does not want, if we do that, it is offence. Do you follow?

Devotee: Yes.
Śrīla Śrīdhar Mahārāj: That He is Autocrat, means He is not under any law, rather His will is law.

The Flow of the Lord's Sweet Will

Śrīla Bhakti Siddhānta Saraswatī Prabhupāda told me in order to show the difference between karma and bhakti,[1] that if a Vaiṣṇava has ordered me, "Give me a flower", and I am bringing a flower to him, and then he says, "No. No flower, give me water", and I say, "O, you already asked for a flower, take it!" – that will be karma, it is to push our will on him.[2] But the Lord is Autocrat, He can do and undo. He desired something, and as a servant I was supplying that, but now He does not want that, so I must stop there. I cannot say, "O, You asked for this item first, and with great energy I have collected it, so You must take it." No! He is Autocrat, He is free, and His free-will is over all. I am nitya-dāsa, His eternal slave. My position is always to serve Him without consideration of law or anything else. He is Autocrat, Absolute Good. Whatever He wants, that is all-in-all. Whatever He has told at one time, He can change. In the śāstra, also He has said:

ājñāyaivaṁ guṇān doṣān
mayādiṣṭān api svakān
dharmān santyajya yaḥ sarvān
māṁ bhajet sa cha sattamaḥ
(Śrīmad Bhāgavatam: 11.11.32)[3]

Who is the best devotee? "One who can understand that in the śāstra I have given so many orders, still, to satisfy Me, one who can neglect those orders already given and can understand what

I want, and come to satisfy Me crossing the directions of the śāstra – he is the best of all devotees."

The Master's Eye

So, it is not a sterilised thing.[4] What we are approaching, what we are going to deal with, it is not anything under law. He is the law-maker, and His will is everything. He said "Let there be water" and there was water, and "Let there be light" and there was light.[5] He is the Cause of all causes, and He is living, and whatever is His desire at any moment, we want to do that. The first-class servant will always look to his Master's eye, and whatever He desires, in the very moment, he will do that. What He has ordered in the past, He can cancel. He gave that order, and He can cancel it and give a new one, and whatever He will desire from us at the present moment, we shall do that, up to our death. It is not that what was previously done, the old thing, we shall re-present that to Him – that won't do, that is not devotion proper. Do you follow?

Devotee: To some extent…

Śrīla Śrīdhar Mahārāj: Try to understand. It is a clear thing, it is not abstruse: whatever He has ordered, He can cancel. He can order, and He can cancel the order and give a new order, and that should be done. He has asked a particular section of servitors, "Do this!" then again, "No, do that" and the after-order will stand. This is the case everywhere. Even in the material instance, the State makes a law, and then they may change that law. Similarly, He is the 'Designer and Destiner' of everything. We can't put Him under any law.

We will prepare ourselves with this attitude: "Whatever is His demand, I shall supply that." Here there is no question of any 'law'. Even if the order is issued by He Himself previously, that won't apply on Him, He is not bound by that. So, Kṛṣṇa says: *sarva-dharmān parityajya mām ekaṁ śaraṇaṁ vraja*[6] – "Give up all varieties of religion, and surrender to Me alone" (*Bhagavad-gītā: 18.66*). Whatever was first ordained by Him in the śāstra, "Do this, and this…" now He says, "Give up everything and come to Me, I am above law."

A Healthy and Holy Movement

We should try to make our interest one with the Absolute interest, that of the Lord. Both knowledge and power-exercising[7] come from our separate interest, a consciousness of separate existence from the Lord. Otherwise, in relation to Him, to Kṛṣṇa, there is spontaneous activity – activity without knowledge, like the operating of a computer – and that is *jñāna-sūnya bhakti*. That spontaneous activity is in the proper way, the harmonious way. Harmony, in fact, comes from it. *Jñāna-sūnya bhakti* is itself harmony – they are one and the same.

Real dedication to Kṛṣṇa means such automatic, spontaneous activity. In self-dedication to Kṛṣṇa, there is no possibility of any cheating, or robbing of others, or of any division. There is no calculation there, and so no cause for any complaint, or necessity of 'justice', or of anything of the kind. Only where there is a culprit, a 'judge' is necessary! But in complete dedication to Kṛṣṇa, automatically the movement is going on, smoothly, properly, and harmoniously, without causing any disturbance. It is a healthy and wholesome flow, and no clash can be expected from that. It is a perfect, spontaneous, holy movement.

In that plane of highest dedication, nothing is lacking – everything is there. It is complete. Yet there is movement, and it is sweetly and spontaneously performed, a spontaneous flow of love, perfect and most desirable. It is the most desirable thing, and it is all-good in itself because Kṛṣṇa is all-good in Himself. He is all-good, Absolute Good, so there is no room for any apprehension, suspicion, or any alternative possibility. The flow of love is smoothly going on.

And those who are seen as apparently incompatible with that flow, they are also necessary there, for Kṛṣṇa's own purpose, for His līlā, because that 'opposition' is motivated by love, just as the mother is seen to apparently punish the child, but in the background that is motivated by her goodwill for the child. So, Yaśodā is chastising her son. She is chasing Him with a stick – such cruelty – and the Absolute is afraid. He is crying! But it is līlā. There is no animosity, no feeling of animosity – it is all the outcome of love.

The Harmony of Dynamic Equilibrium

Such movement is harmless, but not merely harmless, it is health-producing, wholesome. What is 'harmless' we may think of as an equilibrium, but if equilibrium can be dynamic yet producing no disturbance, that is real harmony. Harmony then, is movement but possessing the innocence of equilibrium – and that is healthy.

Devotee: Bhakti is a gift, but at the same time, some subjective endeavour is necessary…

Śrīla Śrīdhar Mahārāj: Gift of whom?

Devotee: Gift of the Super-Subjective…

Śrīla Śrīdhar Mahārāj: Bhakti is self-existent. It is self-existent with God, with Bhagavān. It is His function, His nature, His halo. Bhakti is intrinsically pertaining to Him, co-existent with Him. He is the Whole, the original Whole, and that is an 'Organic Whole', different potencies are existing within it. It is not that some part is 'producing' another; it is an eternal, organic, harmonious organism. That is the Absolute.

Hare Kṛṣṇa, Gaura-Haribol!

Endnotes to Chapter 17

1 *Karma*: Fruitive action. Activity performed with the desire for the fruit, which bears a reaction.
Bhakti: Activity performed for the service and satisfaction of the Lord.

2 As Śrīla Śrīdhar Mahārāj is describing in this chapter, the Lord is not under any 'law' scriptural or social, as if He had been 'voted into power' by the people and so is responsible to satisfy them, to serve their (imagined) interest, such as is the supposed ideal in democracy. But He is not democrat, He is Autocrat: by Himself and for Himself. In this example of the offering of a flower or water to a Vaiṣṇava, the Vaiṣṇava (particularly or specifically the higher Vaiṣṇava) is understood as a manifestation or representation of the Lord, so his wish is similarly independent, not under 'law'.

3 "A saintly person perfectly understands that the ordinary religious duties prescribed by Me in various Vedic scriptures possess favourable qualities that purify the performer, and he knows that neglect of such duties constitutes a discrepancy in one's life. Having taken complete shelter at My lotus feet, however, a saintly person ultimately renounces such ordinary religious duties and worships Me alone. He is thus considered to be the best among all living entities." *(Śrīmad Bhāgavatam: 11.11.32).*

4 "Not a sterilised thing" – the Lord's will, His wish, is law, and He can change it at any moment. It is not always the same, repetitive and predictable. (Śrīla Śrīdhar Mahārāj also used the word 'stereotyped' which carries a similar meaning.)

5 See *Holy Bible, Book of Genesis*, Chapter 1, vv. 3 to 8.

6
sarva-dharmān parityajya
mām ekaṁ śaraṇaṁ vraja
ahaṁ tvāṁ sarva-pāpebhyo
mokṣayiṣyāmi mā śuchaḥ
(Śrīmad Bhagavad-gītā: 18.66)

"Give up all kinds of religion and surrender to Me alone. I will liberate you from all sins, do not despair."

Commenting on this verse, Śrīla Śrīdhar Mahārāj writes: "If one comes to this conception, everything else will be seen as sin (*Ahaṁ tvāṁ sarva-pāpebhyo, mokṣayiṣyāmi*). Everything conceived of as duty or purity in this material world will be seen as sinful, and all conceptions of religiosity will be reduced to the level of sin. In the absolute plane, everything and everyone belongs wholly to Kṛṣṇa, and the slightest deviation from this ideal is no better than committing sin. Mere self-forgetfulness leads to impersonalism and culminates in deep slumber. But self-forgetfulness *(sarva-dharmān parityajya)* in Kṛṣṇa's service (*Mām ekaṁ śaraṇaṁ vraja)* is positive and living. It is the full, absolute plane of life."

(Note: Please see Śrīla Śrīdhar Mahārāj's edition of *Śrī Gītā, The Hidden Treasure of the Sweet Absolute*, for his complete commentary on this verse.)

7 Jñāna, and karma, respectively.

Sri Chaitanya Saraswat Math Book List

These are some of the many books and magazines published in English by Sri Chaitanya Saraswat Math and its spiritually affiliated branches world-wide.

For more information on these and other publications in over twenty languages, please visit the Sri Chaitanya Saraswat Math website at **www.scsmath.com.**

Books by Srila Sridhar Maharaj

Srimad Bhagavad-gita — The Hidden Treasure of the Sweet Absolute
Sri Sri Prapanna Jivanamrtam — Positive and Progressive Immortality
Sri Sri Prema Dhama Deva Stotram
Search for Sri Krishna, Reality the Beautiful
Sri Guru and His Grace
The Golden Volcano of Divine Love
Loving Search for the Lost Servant
Subjective Evolution — The Play of the Sweet Absolute
The Guardian of Devotion
Sermons of the Guardian of Devotion [I-IV]
Home Comfort
Inner Fulfillment
Holy Engagement
The Golden Staircase
Absolute Harmony
Centenary Anthology
Ocean of Nectar

Books by Srila Govinda Maharaj

Bhagavat Darshan
The Divine Servitor
Dignity of the Divine Servitor
Golden Reflections

continued...

The Benedictine Tree of Divine Aspiration
Divine Guidance
Divine Message for the Devotees
Revealed Truth

Various, published from Sri Chaitanya Saraswat Math

Sri Brahma Samhita — Quintessence of Reality the Beautiful.
(With commentary by Srila Bhakti Vinod Thakur)
Sri Nabadwip Dham Mahatmya
and Sri Nabadwip Bhava Taranga (by Srila Bhakti Vinod Thakur)
Sri Upadeshamritam (with commentaries by Srila Bhakti Vinod Thakur and Srila Bhakti Raksak Sridhar Maharaj)
The Bhagavata (by Srila Bhakti Vinod Thakur)
Sri Chaitanya Mahaprabhu
— His Life and Precepts (by Srila Bhakti Vinod Thakur)
Relative Worlds (by Srila Bhakti Siddhanta Saraswati Thakur)
Sri Chaitanya Saraswati 'The Voice of Sri Chaitanyadev' (magazine)

Plus periodicals and publications in many languages of the world.

Enquiries welcome:

www.scsmath.com
www.scsmathlondon.org
www.bhaktiyogainstitute.com

'The Home of Pure Devotion' from where these holy talks emanated:

Sri Chaitanya Saraswat Math,
Kolerganj, P.O. Nabadwip,
District Nadia, W. Bengal, PIN 741302, India